Delayering
Organizations

Delayering Organizations

How to beat bureaucracy
and create a flexible and
responsive organization

Prof. dr. D. Keuning
drs. W. Opheij

with a contribution by
drs. J. Duyser
drs. T. H. Maas

FINANCIAL TIMES

PITMAN PUBLISHING

PITMAN PUBLISHING
128 Long Acre, London WC2E 9AN

A division of Longman Group Limited

First published in 1993 in Dutch under the title 'Verplatting van Organisaties'
English language edition published in 1994

© Doede Keuning 1994

A CIP catalogue record for this book can be obtained from the British Library.

ISBN 0273 60383 3

Translated by M. Rijs Davies

Phototypeset in Linotron Times Roman
by Northern Phototypesetting Co. Ltd., Bolton
Printed and bound in Great Britain
by Biddles Ltd., Guildford and King's Lynn

The Publishers' policy is to use paper manufactured from sustainable forests.

CONTENTS

PREFACE

A large number of organizations are looking for ways to speed up the process of decision making, to avoid information bottlenecks, to give shape to entrepreneurship, to improve the administrative process and to get the best out of managers and staff. In many cases the choice is made in favour of a flatter organizational structure, which means that the distance between the top and the shop floor has to be shortened by delayering.

In practice, however, there are significant differences between what we call 'delayering at the top' (abolishing the divisional layer) and 'delayering the middle management' (eliminating management layers at departmental, section or workgroup level).

This book provides managers and CEOs with the concepts and tools to realize the process of delayering. It is based around a number of case studies which describe delayering in the top as well as at middle management level, and contains the theory to conceptualize the experiences from these cases. *Delayering Organizations* is equally useful to those wishing to, or able to, influence the current method of organization (personnel managers, management consultants, members of works councils, and members of the Board of Directors) as it provides more insight into, and a better understanding of, the (im)possibilities of delayering.

We take an in-depth look at the ways in which the effectiveness of organizations can be improved by decreasing the number of management layers. The formal organizational structure is one of the perspectives. Strategic leadership, management and performance information, reward systems, resource allocation, key appointments and culture equally play a role in this process.

In Chapter 2 we examine the difference between flat and tall organizations. We set out what we mean by a flat organization and indicate which problems in tall organizations might form an indication for delayering at the top and which ones for delayering of the middle management.

Chapter 3 is comprised of nine case studies. These cases are based on interviews with CEOs and managers, authorized information from participating companies and/or secondary sources. The Akzo, Elsevier, General Electric, Asea Brown Boveri (ABB), and NBM-Amstelland cases describe a delayering at the top. The Douglas Aircraft Corporation (DAC), AEGON, Avéro Verzekeringen and Hoogovens case studies describe the delayering in the middle management ranks. We deal with the external and internal reasons for delayering for each company and indicate which elements are, or will be, delayered. We also describe the measures taken to achieve this. Each case study ends with a discussion of the change process.

In Chapter 4 we discuss the tools a manager has for delayering. Referring back to the cases, we discuss which measures CEOs and managers can take to achieve a flatter and more effective organization. There is a substantial difference in the reasons for delayering, the measures, consequences and the implementation of changes between delayering at the top and delayering of the middle management. In this chapter we also pose a number of questions which managers and CEOs can use as a basis on which to consider whether their organization is effective enough or needs adjustment.

Chapter 5 discusses the delayering process. The cases demonstrate that there is no one, best way to go through the process of delayering. It is, however, possible to give a number of important options and points of special attention.

In the final chapter we go on a *tour d'horizon* along the most important trends, measures and process-orientated subjects. The common theme is 'delayering involves more than just lay-offs'. This chapter, and indeed the entire book, contains reflections from CEOs on this type of reorganization, their personal involvement, their view of what has happened, a look back at (and forward to) critical moments and dilemmas and what was crucial for them. It was important to learn from their experiences, principles and wisdom in terms of lessons to be understood.

This book therefore aims to communicate experiences and best practices to others who might find themselves in comparable situations and are considering important organizational changes, such as delayering their organization, in order to improve organizational effectiveness.

Doede Keuning
Wilfrid Opheij

ACKNOWLEDGEMENTS

The research for this book took place under the supervision of Doede Keuning, Professor of Organization and Management and program director of the postgraduate course in Management Consultancy at the Faculty of Economic Science and Econometrics at the Free University of Amsterdam, and was carried out in co-operation with Wilfrid Opheij, who works as management consultant at Twijnstra Gudde nv, management consultants, in Amersfoort, The Netherlands. Drs J. Duijser, at the time of writing a postgraduate student of business economics, has acted as project secretary and his doctoral thesis, 'A background study of flat structures' has given rise to scientific appendices. T.H. Maas, at the time of the study also employed at Twijnstra Gudde, also contributed to the book. G.M. Haksteen was another member of the research team. The case studies contained in this book are based on research carried out by the research team in collaboration with G.A. van Dee (Director), H.M.J.M. van Gogh (partner) and J.B. Loman (partner) of Twijnstra Gudde.

A number of postgraduate students in Organization and Management of the Free University of Amsterdam did contribute to the study in a seminar dedicated to 'the delayering of organizations'. A number of these students were also involved in collecting and processing the basis information for the cases and we would particularly like to mention Manon van Beek, Martijn van Beek, and Miriam Hooiveld in this context.

The texts have been streamlined by A.J. Duijts (editor), in collaboration with I.M. Bijlsma (secretary), both employed at Twijnstra Gudde. The proof correction and preparation of the index were done by V. Bruijns (secretary at the Free University).

The following companies were involved in the research:

ABB
AEGON
Akzo nv
Avéro Verzekeringen
Douglas Aircraft Company
Elsevier
General Electric
Hoogovens
NBM-Amstelland nv.

The researchers appreciate in particular the personal co-operation of K.J. Storm (Member of the Management Council AEGON), A.A. Loudon (Chairman Management Council Akzo), M.A.Th. Jacometti RA (Chairman of Central Management Avéro Verzekeringen), Robert H. Hood Jr. (President DAC), John McDonnell jr. (Chairman and CEO of McDonnell Douglas Corporation), P.J.

Vinken (Chairman Management Council Elsevier), A. Baar (Chairman Management Council NBM-Amstelland) and P. van Rijn (Director Development Operational Management Hoogovens). Largely through their assistance it was possible to interview other managers of these companies. The research team is also grateful to them for their contributions.

The case studies on ABB and GE have been written using material in the public domain, such as annual reports, interviews, books, etc. The text of the GE case study was commented on by George Jamison (Manager of International Communications, General Electric).

The study which this book reports on was supervised on behalf of the commissioning body, the Foundation for Management Studies, by a committee which consisted of the following people: H.J. Brouwer (*Chairman*) Treasurer General of the Ministry of Finance, J.G. Boerlijst, Professor of organizational psychology at the University of Twente, W. Dijkema, Directeur GITP bv, D.J.B. van der Leest, associate Coopers & Lybrand, Dijker van Dien, A.M. Messing, General Manager Dutch Railways nv, B. van Dijkum-de Jong (*Secretary*), Foundation for Management Studies.

The co-operation of the members of the supervisory committee and the management of the Foundation for Management Studies has been greatly appreciated.

Final responsibility for the content of the book rests entirely with the authors.

1

WHAT IS THE EFFECT ON MANAGERS OF THE DELAYERING 'TREND'?

The management of a large number of organizations is looking for ways to accelerate decision-making processes, to avoid information bottlenecks, to give shape to entrepreneurship, to improve the way in which the organization is run, and to get the best out of their managers and employees. In many instances they choose to reduce the distance between 'top and shop floor', to delayer their organization.

In this chapter we will look at some examples of delayering and the underlying trends that can lead to delayering. We will also examine the reasons managers do, or do not, decide to work towards a flatter organization.

DELAYERING IS ON THE INCREASE

In a large number of organizations, delayering is one of the most important organizational changes they will experience. The management ranks and organizational structure of the Douglas Aircraft Company (DAC) were changed drastically in February 1989. The seven levels of management were pared down to five levels. The previous 245 executives positions were cut to 80 and the centralized support organizations were broken up and made permanent parts of each of the aircraft programmes. The move gave each programme the specialist resources it needed to do its work.

At AEGON's subsidiaries, the number of management layers was reduced from five to three. At the same time the way in which the company was organized and the role of managers was changed.

At Hoogovens the Master Plan concentrated on cost reduction, quality, customer orientation, and quality of labour. Part of the change process at Hoogovens was and is a reduction of the number of management layers.

In a large number of merged concerns we see that the positions at the top are reshuffled after a while. This often involves losing a management layer. Asea Brown Boveri (ABB) started immediately after the merger with a large-scale reorganization and integration. Here too, the number of management layers has reduced drastically with time. Percy Barnevik, CEO of ABB, created a corps of just 250 global managers to lead 210,000 employees. At Akzo the reorganization took rather a long time. As a first step, the business units were set up. After they had become independent, the top structure was reorganized so that the Management Council would be able to manage them more directly. This led to a reduction in the number of management layers. The Elsevier concern, which merged in 1979 with NDU, went through a reorganization as early as 1982 when it reduced the number of management layers in the top.

The fact that the delayering trend is on the increase can be deduced from the large number of articles published on the subject. Box 1.1 displays a number of article headlines illustrating this.

Noticing the trend to delayering organizations is one thing. Deciding to follow this trend or to react in any other way to external developments is another matter. It is a decision which is best taken when it is known what is involved. Which underlying reasons do managers have to adjust their organization? What are the advantages? How have other organizations tackled the delayering process? What actions are required?

DELAYERING DOES NOT STAND ON ITS OWN

When looking for the reasons managers have to change their organization, it appeared that the main problems within organizations often occur as a result of changes in their environment. A description of these problems is given below.

Examples of problems

A number of organizations involved in a merger showed little sign of having realized any co-ordination and synergy on completion of the merger. The separate business units still worked alongside, or even in competition with, each other. Elsevier and NBM-Amstelland decided to improve the way in which the top management operated. In the case of NBM-Amstelland this

Box 1.1   Delayering is the focus of attention

The top is being pruned

Will 300,000 managers lose their jobs?

Companies benefit from autonomous task groups

The consequences of a disappearing middle management

"Middle management can expect some heavy blows"

And now it's the turn of the chiefs

How to flatten your organization

led to a much clearer grouping of the various business units.

In the case of ABB and Elsevier, the next step was to improve control from the top. At Elsevier this resulted in the abolition of the divisional layer. At ABB it led to a fundamental change in the way in which the organization was managed and a spectacular reduction in the number of managers.

Another frequent consequence of mergers is the duplication of managerial staff. We often find one layer of staff just below the Management Council, one at divisional level and another one at the level of the business units. This causes communication to slow down and creates an excess of filters in the decision-making process. These various levels of staff furthermore contain highly qualified, and therefore expensive, people whose value added is not always obvious. At ABB, the headquarters staff was cut drastically following the merger in 1987: to 200 from 4,000 in Baden, in the US from 900 to 88, in Germany (Mannheim) from 1,600 to 100, and in Finland (Stromberg) from 880 to 25. US acquisition Combustion Engineering based in Stemford was advised to reduce its staff from 600 to 100. Asea had a headquarters staff of 2000 people in Baden before the merger. The combined company now has a headquarters staff of 150 in Zurich.

AEGON and DAC found that their internal structure caused problems when trying to improve flexibility and quality. Lack of market orientation and co-ordination were therefore important reasons for adjusting the organization. Partly because middle management consisted of too many layers it became difficult to bring products in line with market requirements.

When discussing this precise issue with managers of merged organizations, the term 'maintenance arrears' arose a number of times. They pointed out that, partly because of the merger, not enough attention had been paid to the way in which middle management operated. Not until several years after the merger was there time for a critical look at the value added of the various layers of middle management. Other organizations had also seen a steady increase in the number of managerial positions over the last few years. When business is going well, there is obviously less need to scrutinize the growth of the internal organization. Delayering is an excellent way to reduce slack resources and to overhaul these arrears in maintenance. Percy Barnevik makes sure that a merger or acquisition does not lead to these 'maintenance arrears'. He tends to act quickly and decisively.

ABB, GE, Elsevier, and Akzo have attempted to make their middle management and business units more entrepreneurial and more result-orientated. In a number of situations this was a reaction to the large degree of collective responsibility in middle management, which meant that the result of each individual layer was not obvious. In Chapter 2 we will take a closer look at these problems.

Underlying trends in the environment

When looking at those underlying trends in an organization's environment which can lead to operational problems, managers point time and again to the developments outlined in Figure 1.1. These developments often make it necessary for the organization to adjust.

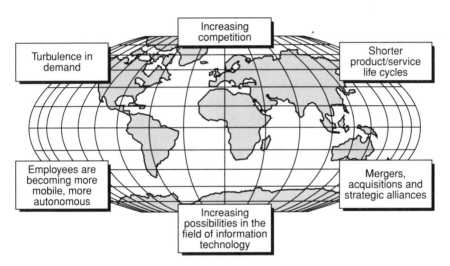

Figure 1.1   Trends in the external environment

Increasing competition

In a number of markets there is evidence of increasing competition. Over-capacity at Hoogovens led, for instance, to fierce competition in which reducing costs was vitally important. In the world of insurance where the money used to 'blow in through the cracks in the door', in a manner of speaking, competition is equally on the increase. A reduction in the product life cycle has led organizations such as AEGON and Avéro Verzekeringen to increase their efforts in the area of product development. In a number of situations, such as for instance at Elsevier, GE and ABB, attention is furthermore focused on global markets where competition is also on the increase.

Shorter product/service life cycles

New technologies follow each other at an ever higher pace. This means that products become obsolete more quickly. Organizations therefore see themselves forced to continuously improve existing products or develop new ones. Because of this reduction in the product life cycle they are barely able to earn back the often high development and production costs. They have to be able to react quickly and with great flexibility to new technological and market developments in order to stay ahead of their competitors. One of the managers interviewed stated, 'What matters is to be the first in the market and to be the fastest to serve your customers: time-based competition'.

The reduction of the product life cycle forces organizations to take down the remaining barriers between R&D, Production, and Marketing in order to stimulate direct communication between them and to clarify the individual contributions. At DAC this was the reason to take down the 'silos'. Looking back, Mr Hood, President of DAC, said, 'Under conditions of severe market pressure we had to do a turnaround in DAC . . . We had to throw the cards, to take apart the functional organization and throw this house of cards together in a revolutionary process and rework the whole . . .'

Mergers, acquisitions and strategic alliances

In order to be able to afford the high development costs and operate on a world-wide scale, many organizations tend to start co-operating in alliances or even merge. Within the resulting big concerns a movement towards decentralization develops. Autonomous units are necessary to guarantee proper decision making despite the large scale. ABB is the best example of a large concern which has fundamentally and structurally decentralized following a merger.

Increasing possibilities in the field of information technology

The increasing possibilities in the field of information technology offer the opportunity to improve efficiency. Developments in the area of networks and management information systems have enabled improved support for decentralized decision making while telecommunications and management information systems provide the means for maintaining a central overview. In order to make optimum use of these possibilities organizations inevitably have to adapt.

Employees are becoming more mobile and more autonomous

The needs patterns of employees change: there is a trend towards increased involvement and more autonomy. Employees wish to have a say in the allocation of work and are also prepared to change jobs (flexibilization). Many employees would like their jobs to become more varied and more involved. The consequence of all this is that managing the mobility and quality of employees has become an important issue (69). At Hoogovens the quality of work is one of the issues to be realized through the implementation of their Master Plan.

Particularly in information-intensive organizations such as AEGON and Avéro Verzekeringen, managers do indicate that all knowledge and skills of well-trained employees are relevant. They therefore tend to work increasingly within wider task-orientated teams. Because these teams are responsible for a large proportion of a job the number of management layers decreases.

One of the managers we interviewed at DAC stated, 'Multi-disciplined teams were primarily operating at the business unit level, one level up from the bottom ring of management . . . The MD-80 programme had about 30 business units with anywhere from 50 to a few hundred multidisciplined members, depending on their mission and location . . . Such teams were much more powerful than employees at the same management level were in the old structure, under which managers had responsibility for only a single discipline'.

In some organizations we see a differentiation of the various career paths so that the various roles (entrepreneur, manager, technical expert) can be rewarded in different ways.

Turbulence in demand

Consumer behaviour changes ever faster and consumer needs are becoming more and more varied. Organizations are thus forced to provide the different consumer groups with variations of the same product. They also need to react more and more quickly to changes in taste and preferences. At Avéro this has led to the creation of several different business units for different groups of clients. One of the business units, FBTO, targets customers wishing to take care of their insurance themselves by means of direct writing. Avéro Life and Damage works mainly through inter-mediaries while Avéro Pensions looks mainly after company pensions. Each of the business units is thus able to work faster and develop better products for their specific target group of customers.

Because of an increasing turbulence in demand organizations wanting to survive into the twenty-first century have to operate close to the market. In trying to structure their organization companies have to work from the outside inwards; the market structure or the customer base dictates the design of the organizational structure. Communication with the client is more direct and no longer hampered by lengthy internal procedures. All this has led to flexible, decentralized, and often flat, units with far reaching responsibilities working for important customers (account groups).

THE ADVANTAGES OF DELAYERING

Solving problems and reacting to trends are not the only motivation for delayering. When listening to executives and managers explaining why they opted to delayer their organizations the reasons mentioned are efficiency; increasing the employees' scope and therefore satisfaction; adapting to the needs of external stakeholders; and the possibility to react in a more flexible and competitive way to external circumstances: dynamic self-preservation.

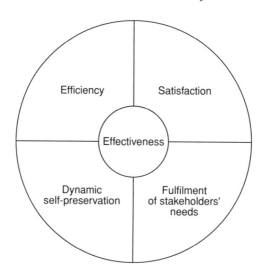

Figure 1.2   Effectiveness criteria

These considerations are displayed in Figure 1.2. In our opinion they all lead to a more effective organization (41).

In Box 1.2 we have given a summary of the effectiveness criteria. We have also indicated to which component of 'organizations' these criteria were connected.

Box 1.2   Organization and effectiveness criteria

Components	*Effectiveness criteria*
Means	**Efficiency** i.e. the degree to which a set goal is achieved sacrificing a minimum of means
Internal participants (organization members)	**Satisfaction** i.e. the degree to which needs of members of the organization are met by means of labour-intrinsic and labour-extrinsic factors
External stakeholders (partners in the societal environment)	**Fulfilment of stakeholders' needs** i.e. the degree to which demands and needs of stakeholders from the external societal environment are met.
The organization as a system which needs to adapt to changes in the environment – third parties, situations – in order to survive in the short and long term	**Self-preservation** through: – flexibility – responsiveness i.e. the degree to which, c.q. the speed with which, an organization can adjust its short-term strategy, structure and operational goals in reaction to changing external circumstances.

Efficiency

Efficiency means achieving maximum results with a minimum of means. Elsevier delayered its organization as early as 1982. When asked whether this has actually increased efficiency the answer was, 'It has, indeed!'

And we can see that the operational income per employee has improved faster in the years 1983, 1984 and 1985 than in other years. These results continue to improve, partly because it is one of the factors used by the Management Council to assess the performance of the business units.

It is very well possible to reduce overheads through delayering. The number of often well-remunerated management posts will decrease. This might result in the remaining management posts requiring a higher remuneration, but, on balance, it is possible to achieve an overall reduction in the cost of wages. Statistical evidence indicates that this reduction can be substantial (69). In the Netherlands it appears, however, that the advantages of these savings can only be realized in the longer term. It therefore becomes all the more important to develop a long-term vision and strategy in this area. Savings can lead to a reduction in prices, an increase in wages, or an investment in human resources/talent. In the long term it can lead to increased competitiveness. It is vital, though, to redefine employee responsibilities when adapting the organization.

Satisfaction

A manager of one of Avéro Verzekeringen's newly formed business units mentioned that most people seem to like working for a small entity with its own characteristics. Most employees also appreciate the increased scope of their employment and their greater involvement in determining and realizing new plans.

Another manager observed, 'If people end up doing the same thing all day long they turn into zombies; this is not practical when the organization is becoming more and more knowledge-intensive'. All managers with whom we discussed this issue also mentioned that some people are, of course, less happy with the increase in responsibility that accompanies the delayering of an organization. The managers concerned did indicate, however, that it was their aim to develop an organization in which people could express their opinions.

Satisfying the needs of stakeholders

ABB was mostly concerned with knowing its customers locally . . . 'Think global, act local' . . . is one of its slogans. By operating geographically close to the customer ABB is 'customer pulled' instead of 'technology pushed'.

AEGON thought it important to change from an extremely bureaucratic insurance company into a company providing high-quality services to customers. In DAC one of its executives pointed out . . . 'Culturally, our company was a strongly hierarchical organization of people with a fierce pride – bordering on arrogance – in their technical and engineering excellence. We did not always listen to what the customer had to say before telling them what they wanted' . . .

Other external stakeholders such as shareholders do also keep a close eye on the organization's management. Elsevier has, for instance, provided shareholders with an excellent return on their investments, especially following its delayering process.

Flexibility and responsiveness

In many cases the delayered organization is better able to react quickly to developments in the market. One manager indicated that delayering had halved the time required to develop new products: 'Because the structure of the organization has been changed it is now possible to make a decision on any subject within a week'. At Elsevier we see that shortening the communication lines and speeding up the decision-making processes were important reasons for delayering. When managers are spread out over a number of layers it is, after all, often impossible to act quickly. The management layers form a filter for the information flow, but if the number of layers is too large the filter gets blocked and this causes delays in the decision-making process.

A computational example

We have developed an example of an organization in the financial services sector which employs c. 15,000 people. Figure 1.3 gives a graphic representation of this example (68). By reducing the number of hierarchical levels it is possible to realize a financial saving of c. 35 per cent on 'management costs'. Because the responsibility and authority of managers will increase, it is realistic to increase their salaries. After all the demands on managers do increase as well. It is usually not until the longer term that these savings are actually realized. Exactly because of this long-term aspect it is necessary to develop a vision and strategy in this area.

WHY NOT SIMPLY START

Considering that delayering leads to greater efficiency, that employees prefer it, that it enables us to provide a better service to external parties

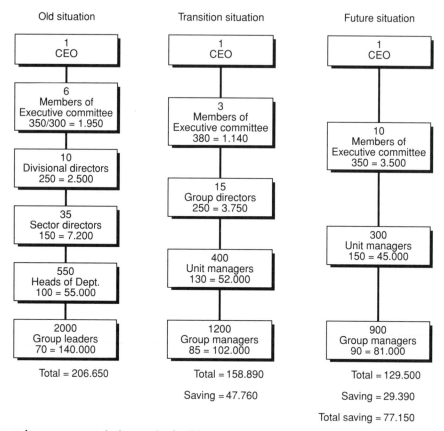

- Average amounts in thousands of guilders
- Hypothetical example based on companies in the financial services sector in the Netherlands
- Not included are the substitution effects in increased staff costs and an increase in responsibilities of jobs on the shop floor

Figure 1.3   Improved returns by means of delayering

and that it makes companies more competitive and react with greater flexibility to external developments, why didn't everybody start the delayering process yesterday? There are obviously reasons why not.

The number of layers within the organization is already limited

One of the reasons why delayering is not worth considering is a very simple one. In conversation with a manager of a company which manufactures sensitive mechanical equipment it appeared that this particular organization already was as flat as the proverbial pancake. The company had always guarded against introducing too many hierarchical layers.

It had always operated in a very competitive market. This meant paying a great deal of attention to the relation between direct and indirect employees. Furthermore, market-orientated teams which had a large degree of collective responsibility for product development, production, after-sales service and contribution to the trading result, had been a feature of this company since the 1960s.

One of the factors which determines the effectiveness of an organization is the number of management layers. This is illustrated in Figure 1.4

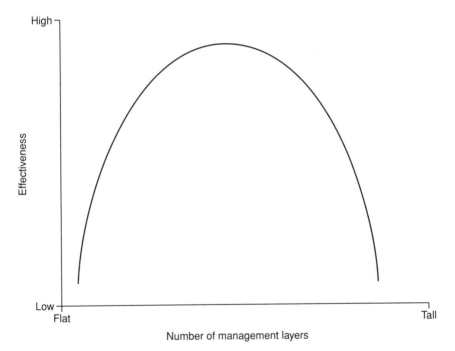

Figure 1.4   There is an optimum number of management layers

There is obviously an optimum situation: when an organization is too hierarchical it is not efficient, but when it is too flat there are other problems. It is almost impossible to give general guidelines as to where the optimum lies. It very much depends on, for instance, the size of the organization, the nature of its operations, and a number of other factors. We will come back to this in Chapter 2.

Other solutions can prove equally adequate

The demands that the environment places on an organization can be met in a number of ways. In particular, solutions might be found at any of the following levels (see Figure 1.5): strategic level (setting goals), operational level (realization), organizational level (organization).

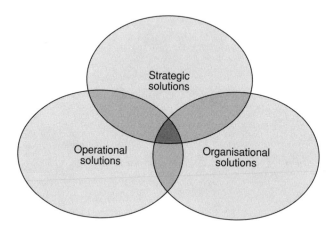

Figure 1.5   Possible solutions for improving effectiveness

At a strategic level an organization can opt to devise a strategy that is more in line with recent developments in its markets. Some examples of possible strategic solutions are: diversification, which is expanding or moving an organization's operations into different markets or market sectors; cost-leadership, which is aiming to achieve the lowest cost in comparison to the competition; globalization, which is taking production and distribution to a global level. Improving effectiveness is also receiving a large amount of attention at an operational level ('on the shop floor'). In particular, the factors 'efficiency' and 'satisfaction' are used to improve overall effectiveness. Examples of solutions in this area are quality processes, training, cost-reduction programmes and integral process improvements (work-flow management).

Solutions at an organizational level mainly involve the way in which the organization is run. This means that the tasks, authority and responsibilities of the management change. We are, in fact, talking about changes to the structure of the organization. The various structural solutions for improving effectiveness are (see Figure 1.6):

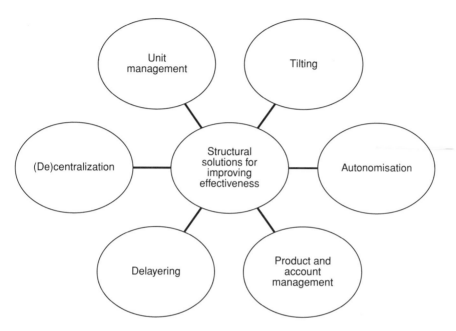

Figure 1.6   Structural solutions for improving effectiveness

- (de)centralization, which is moving tasks, authority and responsibilities upwards or downwards in the organization, which also gives the opportunity to change the 'composition' of the various layers of management;
- unit management, which is the introduction of separate units who are responsible for results realignment;
- tilting the organization, which is reorientation of the organization (from a functional to a product, geographic and/or market orientation);
- autonomization, which is developing part of the organization into an independent company;
- product and account management, which is introducing customer-orientated units co-ordinating activities regarding important clients or product-orientated units co-ordinating activities relating to certain products.

Another structural solution is delayering. This is the solution we will concentrate on.

Delayering is a complex process

It appears simple but, as we shall see, delayering is a process which has an impact on a great many aspects of a business. It may seem that delayering is a transformation which only affects the structure of an organization, but, for it to succeed, a number of other changes are required.

Delayering requires a different type of leadership based on 'entrepreneurship' and not all managers can cope with this. We should not forget either that the set-up of information systems in delayered organizations varies quite drastically from those in non-delayered organizations. While technology offers a great many possibilities, it is obvious that these systems cannot be changed overnight. Furthermore, employees will have to see an increase in responsibility and a wider job description as a challenge and experienced managers know that not everyone will muster the same enthusiasm for this.

Decentralization of authority and a committed investment in certain business units (thereby excluding others) can also have a negative effect on the delayering decision. Confidence in the qualities and abilities of employees (or, when these are lacking, a readiness to invest in them) is a prerequisite for the success of the delayering process. While most managers and administrators preach this confidence, in practice they are born 'centralists'. Finally, delayering requires a change of culture, leading by example from the top and a change in behaviour from managers and employees. This often turns out to be a slow and laborious process. Managers who realize what delayering involves often think twice before deciding to proceed with the process. The risk exists that the following question will pop up, 'Have we really managed to lose some layers or is it only job titles that have disappeared?'

New disadvantages

Delayering does not only have advantages, it also entails some disadvantages. Every choice of company structure is only ever a 'temporary compromise'. Every option entails its own disadvantages. It is important to recognize these disadvantages in advance and to ensure that they are compensated for as much as possible. In this book the advantages and disadvantages of the various company structures will be discussed.

In order to stop a delayering operation from going too far it is essential to recognize the dysfunctions of a flat structure, so that the length of hierarchy of a structure can continuously be adjusted and optimized. We list a few examples of potential new disadvantages.

In a flat structure, the risk exists that the organization becomes *myopic*. The units of the flat organization only concentrate on short-term results within their product-market combination. Consequently, too few strategic decisions are made.

Another risk is the occurrence of a *responsibility crisis*. The stress on management is too great. The people at the top compete with each other for attention. The excess responsibilities can lead to stress, illness, excessively prescriptive behaviour and additional insecurity reduction by excessive engagement of advice.

The *decision-making process* can also be *frustrated* by too flat a structure. This may seem a paradox at first glance, but the explanation is that decisions are not (re)evaluated enough by objective parties. There is also a risk of excessive consultation because too many people are involved in the decision-making process.

The organization can become so flat as to become 'disjointed'. Each unit only sees its own interests and there is no synergy.

Finally, too flat an organization can become *inefficient* because of a duplication of staff, management, and production means.

HOW CAN THIS BOOK BE OF USE TO THE READER

This book offers the reader a handle on the delayering process. It will also provide an insight into the possibilities and impossibilities of delayering for those who wish to or can influence the organizational set-up, such as personnel directors, consultants, members of the works council or the Board of Directors. We will discuss the possibilities for increasing the effectiveness of an organization by decreasing the number of management layers. The organizational structure is only one of the angles. We will also consider leadership, performance information, remuneration problems, budget allocation, personal interpretation and culture.

In Chapter 2 we will consider the difference between flat and tall organizations. We will discuss what we understand by a flat organization and give an indication of which problems in the tall organization may give rise to a delayering of the top and of the middle management.

Chapter 3 consists of nine case studies. These case studies are based, in the main, on interviews with managers and sources in the public domain. In the case of Akzo, Elsevier, General Electric, ABB and NBM-Amstelland we discussed the delayering of the top. In the case of DAC, AEGON, Avéro Insurance and Hoogovens we discuss the delayering of the middle management. In each case we will outline the external and internal reasons for delayering.

We will then describe what has been or will be delayered and indicate which actions have been taken. The final part of each case will consist of a description of the change process. The cases offer the reader the possibility to take a peek behind the scenes of nine organizations. They are not meant to form the basis of scientific conclusions, but merely serve as an illustration of the theories outlined in this book.

In Chapter 4 we will consider the instruments for delayering. Looking back to the cases we point out what actions can be taken to ensure a flatter and more effective organization. We will also pose a number of questions which can be used to assess whether an organization is sufficiently effective or whether it needs to adjust.

In Chapter 5 the delayering process is discussed in more detail. The cases already illustrate that there is no one, best way for the process of delayering. It is however possible to indicate a number of options and points for consideration.

In the final chapter we take a 'bird's-eye view' of the major trends, measures and process-orientated subjects. The common theme is 'delayering means more than just lay-offs?'.

In the appendices you will find a short description of the scientific research into delayering.

Appendix 1 is concerned with national cultures: why is delayering so relevant in, for instance, The Netherlands? Appendix 2 contains a summary of a number of studies into the relation between performance, satisfaction and the number of management layers.

2

WHAT DOES DELAYERING ACTUALLY MEAN?

When choosing to reduce the distance between 'top and shop floor' we come across terms such as 'the number of management layers', 'decentralization', 'autonomy', 'manageability' and 'span of control'. Changing the structure on its own will hardly lead to any improvement at all. This requires much more.

In this chapter we will not only look at the characteristics of a flat organization, but also at factors that contribute to flatter structures actually leading to improvement. We will further pay attention to those problems which are an indication for delayering at the top and those which are an indication for delayering of the middle management layers.

WHAT CONSTITUTES A FLAT ORGANIZATION

When we are talking about delayering we are referring to *the process in which the number of management layers in an organization is reduced.*

In this section we will discuss those interrelated factors which contribute to a fully functioning flat organization. We will thus first need to establish what the characteristics of a flat structure are. However, delayering is more involved than simply changing an organization's structure and we will therefore also look at other measures in the delayering process.

Characteristics of a flat structure

The delayering process involves changing the structure of an organization. We will first define what we mean by structure. This definition will then form the basis for further discussions of flat and tall structures.

When talking about structure we are not, in the first instance, referring to the organizational scheme – although in practice this has an important role to play – but to the elements set out in Box 2.1 (the definition of the organization's structure).

Box 2.1 Definition of organizational structure

- The arrangement of all activities to be carried out via the roles and tasks of individual employees, work groups and departments.

- The defined authority and the relation between individual employees, work groups and departments in carrying out their tasks.

- The in-built channels of communication and mechanisms used by individual employees, work groups and departments to stay in contact for the purpose of providing the necessary direction and co-ordination.

This definition of organizational structure consists of various elements. We use these elements to assess whether a structure is tall or flat. This means that we need to establish first to what extent specialization and differentiation of roles leads to *hierarchical levels*. The number of these levels is closely related to the *scope of control* of management (as a function of the span of control and depth of control). We consider in particular the number of employees one manager can directly or indirectly lead in an effective manner. Because not all operations take place within departments, we will also look at temporary organizational units such as *work and project groups*.

Authority also has a role to play in the definition of the structure; what matters here is the *delegation of authority*. Another important structural factor is co-ordination. It is possible to establish whether managers or heads of departments do co-ordinate and whether this takes place in mutual adjustment. In Box 2.2 we have outlined the structural characteristics of the extremes of flat and tall organizations.

Box 2.2 Extremes of structural characteristics

	Flat	*Tall*
Number of hierarchical levels	Small	Large
Mean scope of control	Large	Small
Number of *ad hoc* work or project groups	Large	Small
Delegation	Much	Little
Co-ordination by means of mutual adjustment	Much	Little

In the paragraphs below we will clarify the characteristics of a flat structure.

A limited number of hierarchical levels, and thus a large scope of control

It is impossible to give exact figures for the optimum number of reporting points and management layers and the corresponding optimum scope of control. Various studies into the number of management layers have been carried out (Appendix 2). It appears that it is not possible to give generally applicable guidelines as to the optimum number of layers. Organization-specific factors, such as branch, age, culture and style of leadership do play an important role. A 1989 international study compared the actual situation in 105 business units (40).

Very generally speaking, the following principles can be distilled from this study:

- organizational units of up to 500 employees tend to be comprised of four layers
- organizational units of between 500 and 1,200 employees are generally comprised of five layers, and of these 70 per cent are comprised of four to six layers
- organizational units of between 1,200 and 4,500 employees are generally comprised of six layers
- organizational units of more than 4,500 employees are generally comprised of seven layers.

In each of these categories we see that organizations engaged in the delayering process pursue the minimum number of levels possible.

The scope of control varies in practice horizontally from four to 25 employees (= span of control) and vertically from one to seven layers (= depth of control). Again, there are exceptions to this rule. Factors which determine the scope of control are:

- expertise and personality of the management
- comparability of the work
- required level of leadership and co-ordination
- complexity of the work
- geographical proximity
- knowledge and experience of employees
- availability of staff support.

Jack Welch stated in this respect in the *Harvard Business Review*:

'Remember the theory that a manager should have no more than 6 or 7 direct reports? I say the right number is closer to 10 or 15. This way you have no choice but to let people flex their muscles, let them grow and mature. With 10 or 15 reports, a leader can focus only on the big, important issues, not on minutial.'

Furthermore, the way in which operations are structured is important. We will return to this in Chapter 4.

An unambiguous main structure within which freedom for ad hoc *structuring exists*

When every new role or every problem gives rise to the need for a new department, the consequence is obviously a tall structure. This is why in flat organizations a large degree of freedom exists to create *ad hoc* structures – for instance, task groups, project groups or temporary departments.

The main structure is fixed but, within it, a certain freedom exists for managers to organize the work in an optimum fashion. There is, however, a snake in the grass. Tall organizations can also have a great many forms of consultation that appear to be temporary. In flat organizations these tasks or project groups are truly temporary; they are disbanded once the assignment is completed and the required results have been achieved.

A large amount of delegation of responsibility and authority

Another essential principle of a flat organization is the large degree of delegation and decentralization of responsibilities and authority.

In several situations, the top management is easily tempted to make decisions regarding relatively minor matters such as employing temporary staff and engaging caterers. Such decisions are best left to a manager further down the line.

Delegation prevents decisions being made by means of a long chain of command. An indication of a long chain of command is if every decision needs to be signed off by a large number of signatories. Every hierarchical level has, after all, its own authority and its own priorities. In a flat organization, managers have, at a decentralized level, more scope to make their own decisions.

A great amount of co-ordination by means of mutual adjustment within as well as between departments

In a flat organization, co-ordination usually takes place through mutual consultation and adjustment. Mutual adjustment can exist within as well as between the departments. Consultation between the units can take shape by laying down mutual agreements by means of contract management. The bottom line is, 'only if we can't agree amongst ourselves will the boss get involved'. The 'lines' will thus not be clogged with matters which can very easily be solved by mutual adjustment.

Delayering involves more than just the structure

Simply changing the structure by reducing the number of management layers does not automatically lead to an increase in the speed with which decisions are made, to energy being concentrated on the enterprise/entrepreneurship, or more attention being paid to the needs of the customers. Managers have several means at their disposition to enhance the effect of a change in structure. These means are displayed in Figure 2.1 and are discussed further below (90). Making changes in these areas are therefore measures which lead to delayering.

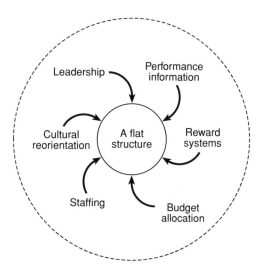

Figure 2.1   Interrelated aspects which contribute to a flat structure

Leadership

Flat organizations place high demands on the style of leadership. Different levels require different styles. At the top level the attention should be focused on those factors which lead to the development and implementation of a successful strategy. Leadership needs to take place at arm's length.

At a *decentralized level* managers are mainly intrapreneurs posing as 'team builders'.

Performance information

Within flat organizations the decision-making process is, to a large extent, decentralized. The top however does need to have an idea of the degree to which competitive advantages and results are achieved. In order for the top management to be accountable they have to be able to see the effects of their decisions. These effects can be made visible by operating a system of justification and reporting which is, in many instances, backed up by an automated system. Apart from processing transactions (keeping a record of the daily operational activities) the systems at a decentralized level also need to assist with the management of and the decision making regarding these activities.

Reward system

In flat organizations, tasks or roles are less important than results. This is expressed in rewards, material or immaterial. Rewarding of individual achievements should, however, never happen at the expense of the team spirit.

The challenge for many organizations wishing to delayer is to find a means of rewarding people which is both flexible and recognizes achievement of results. When the number of management positions decreases, it is important to bind managers and employees to the organization by giving them challenging tasks. The remaining management positions are generally less narrow and therefore more interesting. The new situation also offers employees the prospect of jobs with a more challenging content.

Budget allocation

Important in allocating the budget is, in the first instance, the way in which the budget cycle and allocation of the available investment capacity are organized. A second important element is the freedom the decentralized unit has to act on the basis of strategic choices and the corresponding budget allocation.

On the basis of strategic and tactical plans developed at the decentralized level, budgets are allocated – after decision making by the top. These budgets are to cover investments as well as costs in relation to the turnover to be achieved. Apart from financial indicators more entrepreneurial targets can form part of the mutual agreements. The decentralized units should, themselves, also be able to contract internally or externally.

In a flat structure within which several units operate, it can happen that these different units are looking to realize different strategic goals (for example, unit 1 aims to achieve lowest cost; unit 2 optimal after-sales service). If this is a strategic choice, the allocation of people and means will have to correspond with the priorities set out by the organization as a whole in relation to these different strategic goals.

Staffing

'The right person in the right place' is of essential importance for the flat organization. Not only for the management, but also for employees it is important that a good relationship between the employees, and between employees and management, can develop. In flat organizations the system is not just based on 'promotion on the basis of years in service and along the hierarchical line'. A great deal of attention is paid to gaining relevant experience (job rotation) developing knowledge and skills (training) and regular assessment.

Culture

In flat organizations, a strong cultural development has an essential role to play. The more culture and strategy are in line with each other, the less important are formal guidelines, procedures and direct supervision. Exactly because of the latter, extra management layers or, at least, bureaucratic regulations, often develop. In Figure 2.2 several different types of culture are displayed (30, 80).

An organization hardly ever consists of a 'monoculture'. Characteristics of the various types of cultures often occur alongside each other. What tends to happen is that certain characteristics are more apparent.

In flat organizations, the characteristics of a task- or person-orientated culture tend to dominate. The characteristics of a power- or role-orientated culture are generally less predominant. Internal entrepreneurship and a responsibility for results are largely responsible for the determination of norms and values in a flat organization.

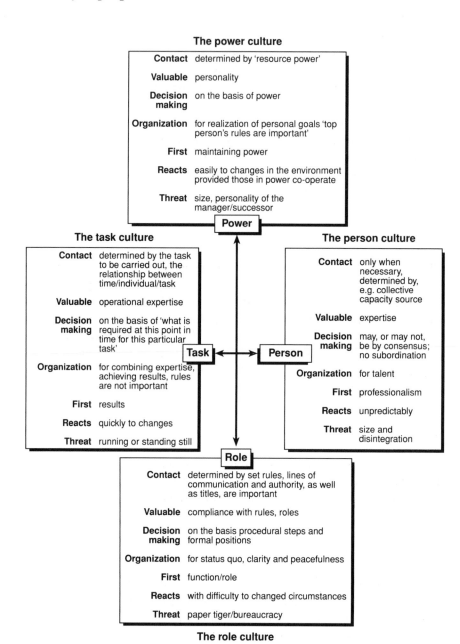

Figure 2.2   Various types of culture

INDICATIONS FOR DELAYERING

Different problems require different solutions. In practice we see some organizations that have a large number of management layers at the top. Others tend to have a strongly hierarchical middle management. It is, of course, also possible for an entire organization, i.e. top as well as middle management, to consist of a large number of management layers.

In this section we will look in more detail at the problems of too tall a top

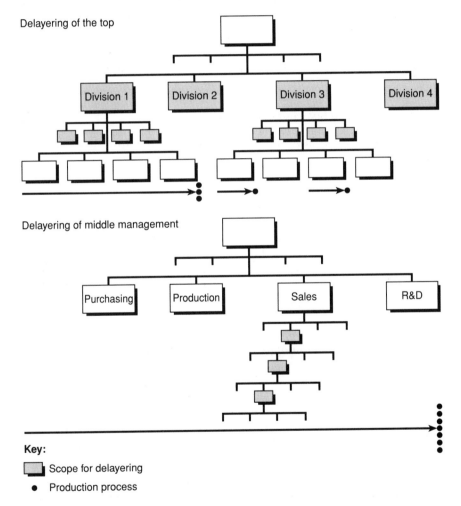

Figure 2.3   Delayering options

and too tall a middle management. It is usually these problems which form the incentive to change. Delayering of the top and delayering of the middle management are two different processes which can each solve different problems. In Figure 2.3 we have indicated where delayering is possible. In the case of too tall a top we find a surplus of strategy developing and co-ordinating management layers. This tends to occur in organizations with a divisional top structure. In between the Board of Management and the business units a number of divisional managers operate, each with their own staff and support services.

In the case of too tall a middle management layer we see a surplus of echelons which is expressed in the number of managers and heads of department in between top management and shop floor. We see this on a regular basis in organizations which are organized by function. The number of middle managers with their own little departments is enormous.

Reasons for the delayering of the top

Organizations which have too tall a top often suffer from the following problems.

Lack of commitment to the realization of plans

The existence of too many layers at the top often makes the implementation of changes and new plans very difficult. They form a buffer between the top and the business units which hinders communication and commitment. This buffer works both ways: it blocks plans developed at the top, but also plans developed in the business units.

Difficulties with division of tasks and responsibilities

Often friction occurs between the concerns of the top, the division and the business unit regarding tasks, responsibilities and authority. Who decides on substantial investment, how are budgets approved, who looks after co-ordination when various business units supply the same customers? The management of decentralized units requires good control of complex tasks and authority, but the top and the intermediate divisions want to maintain some form of overview, co-ordinate and assess units on their performance. The units' response is, you can only assess us on our performance if we can make our own decisions.

Duplication of staff and consultative bodies

Every management layer in the top aims to be as independent and self-sufficient as is possible. In order to achieve this, it is customary to create one's own staff for every division and business unit. This staff supports the manager, checks, advises and is able to dictate ways of operating. The consequence is that several individuals at various levels do the same work. This duplication of staff bodies inevitably results in new forms of consultation. After all, staff have to co-ordinate their work in the area of finance, personnel, logistics, quality and marketing. In many situations we see that each of these functions conflicts with the others because they all demand maximum attention. The staff functions will eventually side with their division or business unit and be selective in what information they pass on to the top. Furthermore, there are some doubts in the subsidiaries or business units as to the value added of the division or staff concerned, in particular, in relation to the often obligatory adjustment of the overheads.

Keeping each other occupied at the top

The complex division of tasks and authorities and the duplication of staff and consultative bodies results in the members of the top being more concerned with each other than with the market and competitors. 'Internal' sales require so much time that genuine entrepreneurs become demoralized. There will, of course, always be managers and staff employees willing to give all their time and efforts to these internal activities. The question is, however, how much added value these activities have.

An exaggerated 'checking urge'

The higher layers often see it as their task to 'protect the more operational managers from their own mistakes'. This, in itself, is not a fault. However, it is more a matter of pulling rank than of authority, knowledge and experience. This type of support is seen by the decentralized managers as interference, an urge to constantly 'check' everything, and resistance.

Delays in decision making

It may be obvious that all the above mentioned problems together lead to substantial delays in the decision-making process. The realization of plans and the implementation of change is endangered. However, external developments mean that relative speed (in relation to competitors) and absolute speed (in relation to clients' expectations) become more and more important. This gives ample reasons for a delayering of the top structure when these problems occur.

Reasons for the delayering of middle management

The problems occurring in organizations with too tall a middle management layer often lead to a reorganization of work processes and co-operation. What follows is an overview of these problems.

Problems concerning market orientation and co-ordination

If companies want to adapt to the ever-changing consumer demands and the market globalization, they need to 'translate' these external changes internally. Organizations with too large a middle management layer are often not in the best position to do so. Middle managers of the marketing department need to go through a number of echelons to communicate with middle managers in the production units. This certainly makes a rapid adjustment of the production processes, as required by the markets, difficult.

Companies often try to find a solution in complicated co-ordination mechanisms and an increase in hierarchical levels between the operational areas of marketing and production. The end result is often total blockage of information channels.

Policy making and execution of operations are too separate

Policy making takes place at the top and is communicated via hierarchical reporting lines to the shop floor. The heads of the various production units are not involved in any way in this process. The top may well formulate strategies but if it then expects everyone to march to the beat of its drum it may be expecting too much. This can mean that a certain strategy lacks the basis it needs, making following this particular strategy extremely difficult.

On the other hand, the risk exists that insights from the shop floor do not filter through to the top. Communication channels which are too long therefore hamper proper policy and decision making.

Too little entrepreneurship and accountability

In organizations with too tall a middle management layer it is not always clear what it is that middle managers should be assessed on. In other words, what should be the result of their department. People often hide behind collective responsibilities. Another factor in this is that, as we saw earlier, a middle management layer which is too tall leads to blockage of information. Information regarding the actual functioning of the shop floor often does not, or only in a filtered form, reach the top.

It often happens that costs are budgeted for but results are not planned for. In particular, efficiency and, therein, the preservation of the company can suffer because of this. Ultimately, it is only the top which is accountable for the results.

Few chances to develop integral management skills

In organizations with too large a middle management layer we often see a lack of managers with general and integral management experience. The development of these skills is not even stimulated. In these organizations a tendency to overspecialize in one area often occurs.

Managers often spring from the 'functional legs' of an organization. Once they reach the top, these managers appear incapable of strategic thinking or of taking the organization as a whole in tow.

Bureaucratic, role-orientated culture

The culture of organizations with too tall a middle management layer is characterized by procedures and shared responsibilities. Furthermore, titles, positions and a place in consultative bodies are given too much importance. In the longer term, this leads to a situation in which the achievements are no longer the main aim, but the gathering of new positions is. The contact with clients is lost and rejuvenating initiatives get stuck in the mud of bureaucratic procedures and consultative bodies.

The problems we have identified all have a negative effect on all aspects of a company's effectiveness.

- *Efficiency* Too large a middle management layer involves enormous costs. Operational costs are furthermore spread out over too many departments and heads of departments.
- *Satisfaction* While die-hard operational experts can still find some satisfaction in the situation, the surplus of middle management stops managers with more general skills in their tracks. It is even the case that the combined skills of thinking and acting which people might have are not being tapped.

- *Satisfying stakeholders' needs* Too wide a middle management layer will eventually have a negative effect on meeting the needs of external parties who are no longer able to get hold of the right person in the many echelons of this cumbersome, bureaucratic organization.
- *Dynamic self-preservation* Flexibility and responsiveness suffer badly from too wide a middle management layer. The ability to change is drastically reduced by clogged communication lines and lack of entrepreneurship.

So, there are different reasons for delayering the top and delayering the middle management layer. As we shall see, the delayering process for each is also different.

3

CASE STUDIES

We discussed the topic of delayering in seven organizations where delayering was or is one of a number of changes taking place. We were particularly interested in the reasons for delayering, the old and the new structure and the other changes that were initiated and carried out. The cases of ABB and GE have been compiled on the basis of information in the public domain.

There are differences in the way in which managers and executives refer to delayering of the top and delayering of the middle management. Both types of delayering have been discussed in several organizations. Delayering of the middle management was discussed with managers and executives of AEGON, Avéro Verzekeringen, Hoogovens and DAC. Delayering of the top was discussed with executives who felt that their divisionally structured organizations did not function as well as they could: GE, Akzo, Elsevier and NBM-Amstelland. ABB went through a delayering of the top as well as the middle management.

Most organizations are still talking about and going through the process of delayering. At Elsevier, however, delayering took place in 1982, a delayering *avant la lettre*. The same goes for GE in 1985.

In organizations where the top was to be delayered, we talked in most cases to the Chairman of the Board of Management about their reasons for delayering, their solutions and their personal agenda. At those organizations which went through a delayering of the middle management, we spoke to the top person as well as a number of managers directly involved in the restructuring of the middle management layer.

The case studies each start with a general overview of the organization. We then look into those factors which, for this specific organization, played an important role in the decision to delayer. The old and new structure, as well as a number of corresponding changes, are discussed. And, finally, we will outline some of the characteristics of the delayering process.

AEGON

This case study describes the delayering process at AEGON, which started in 1989. The process was part of a larger organizational development plan and was targeted at the middle management.

Brief overview

AEGON was formed on 30 November 1983 as a result of the merger between the insurance companies AGO and Ennia. AEGON is a leading international insurance group the headquarters of which are based in The Hague. The business' geographical focus is in the Netherlands and the United States, which are responsible for 57 and 35 per cent of total turnover. The remaining business units are located in Belgium, Greece, Spain, Hungary, the UK and the Caribbean.

Table 3.1 Overview of AEGON's key business statistics from 1986 to 1992

	1986	1987	1988	1989	1990	1991	1992
Turnover*	4,820	5,511	5,818	6,305	6,891	7,642	8,241
Profit*	243	314	389	480	587	594	628
Staff	4,049	3,862	3,736	3,621	3,540	3,468	3,140

*Amounts in millions of guilders

AEGON's product range concentrates on life assurance and related financial products. AEGON are furthermore active in the area of health and accident insurance and property insurance. It is thus a major corporate investor and, as such, involved in a variety of activities. AEGON has a number of subsidiaries which offer specific banking services. For instance, the FGH bank is active on the property market and the Bank Labouchère operates on the stock market and has full banking status.

AEGON furthermore run a number of holiday parks in the Netherlands and Germany. Figure 3.1 displays AEGON's old structure.

External developments

Over the last few years, the financial sector has been characterized by a large degree of turbulence. The most important developments were deregulation, internationalization, differentiation, integration of financial markets, and

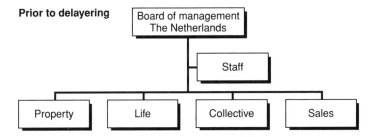

Prior to delayering

Board of management
The Netherlands

Staff

Property · Life · Collective · Sales

Figure 3.1   AEGON's structure prior to delayering

innovation. These developments have led to the abolition of the division between the banking and insurance business and organizations from both lines of business have moved into each other's fields through various forms of co-operation. AEGON have taken a clear stance in these matters; there are no plans to merge with a bank.

In addition to this, the stable image of the insurance world changed drastically in the 1980s. Competition in this market increased, new forms of distribution, such as direct writing gained ground, and foreign insurance companies managed to penetrate the Dutch market. The insurance business had to change course and develop into a more market-orientated organization.

Internal developments

AEGON, too, had to change tack from a highly bureaucratic company to a company offering high-quality services to its customers. This was a gradual process, involving a number of steps which preceded the actual delayering.

The 'themes' of these steps are displayed in Table 3.2 and further explained in the following text.

Merger

In 1983 AGO and Ennia merged to improve their market position and to strengthen the basis for autonomous international expansion.

Integration

The AGO and Ennia organizations were merged, which resulted in 1984 in

Table 3.2 Overview of change themes

Theme	Date	Key word	Reason
Merger	1983	AGO/Ennia	Economies of scale
Integration	1986	AEGON NL	Internal competition
Improvement	1986	'STC'	Market share
Motivation	1987	Management development	Internal intrapreneurship
Decentralization	1989	Delayering	Turnover responsibility

an organizational structure with two profit centres offering the full range of insurance products.

Soon it emerged that a large amount of competition existed between the two companies. Loss of market share and a rise in costs were the consequence of this internal competition. In 1986 a new organization structure was set up. The newly formed business units Property Insurance, Life Assurance, Collective Life Assurance, Mortgages, and Sales were placed under one Management NL with the following administrative departments: Control, Social Services and Automation.

Improvement

From the customers came the indication that AEGON products had to be improved. A plan was developed for the next few years. The message was: Service up, Turnover up, Costs down; in short: STC.

Each business unit was set ambitious targets. It was no longer systems and procedures which mattered, but results. Industrial planning and budgeting were centralized and all sectors had to contribute. In addition to this the Quality concept was introduced at AEGON NL.

For the first time, the primary process was seen as a logical chain of actions that had to be in tune with each other. This caused the management process to change from vertical to horizontal.

Motivation

Heads of departments had to work together in a functional manner and to consider each other as customer and supplier. This process was supported by a large number of activities in the area of quality. In addition to this, 1988 saw the start of an AEGON-wide planned approach to middle management training.

Decentralization

Prior to the transformation process of middle management, business units were decentralized. Everywhere within AEGON NL organizations were 'flattened' by reducing the number of management layers to three.

Delayering

The delayering operation caused some essential structural changes at AEGON. This becomes apparent when looking at the structure before and after delayering.

AEGON's new structure, which came into existence after decentralization, is displayed in Figure 3.2.

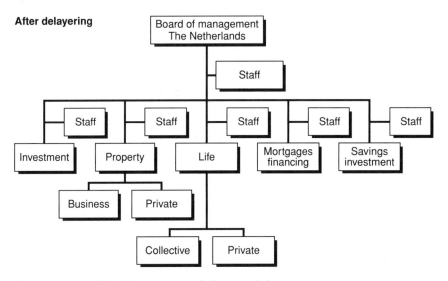

Figure 3.2   AEGON's structure following delayering

The management team has now been organized by function and is responsible for personnel management, financial management, product development and marketing.

Each product group now has its own sales, production and development systems. The heads of department have full responsibility for operations as well as turnover and have a much larger span of control than before. This means that they have autonomous control over a large part of the primary process. They also have a large measure of control in bringing in support services. In consultation with higher management they are responsible for buying in the services of staff departments such as Personnel and Automation.

Because the number of hierarchical layers is reduced, the lines have become shorter (Figure 3.3).

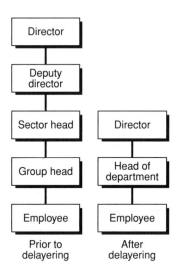

Figure 3.3   Short lines as a result of delayering at AEGON

Setting up the units reduced the number of hierarchical layers. For the majority of units this means that two hierarchical layers have disappeared. Communication and feedback have improved, which results in a faster decision-making process. Employees and first-line managers also feel more involved.

The new role of middle management

Middle management is expected to create space for employees. Providing encouragement and motivation has become more important than control and sanctioning. The energy flow has made a turn; from looking upwards to check whether the boss is happy to looking outwards to check whether the customer is happy. The organization has undergone a radical reorientation.

Where before the top was the boss's place, it is now the customer's; the boss can be found at the bottom, supporting people in the fight for market share.

The heads of department have gained more authority, but they are now also responsible for the results of their departments. In order to be able to assess the results that have to be achieved, performance indicators have been developed.

Heads of departments find themselves faced with the following problems:

1 finding a balance between operating at a people-orientated level and operating at a product-orientated level
2 improving achievements with limited resources and at lower cost.

However, they have gained a better insight into personnel, financial management and automation matters.

Finally, every employee has to realize that the client occupies centre stage; the client has to be satisfied. To this end, various client values such as speed, clarity, sympathy and ease, have been translated into behavioural criteria for employees.

The delayering process

AEGON refers to the process as 'evolutionary with intermittent revolutions'. Evolutionary because it was decided to change gradually. The revolutions were necessary to get the organization on the right track.

During each phase of the process, AEGON's management has played an enthusing and motivating role. In particular, the enthusiasm of the then Chairman of the Board of Management, Mr Storm, has been instrumental in leading the organization successfully through the delayering process.

The discussions which took place were more concerned with the implementation of changes than the need to change. A major problem existed in that the reduction in management positions led to a reduction in the size of the internal job market.

Support for the delayering process came in a number of ways. Quality projects were set up to stimulate the Quality concept within AEGON. After the change in structure, work groups were set up in which the top management and heads of departments could discuss how to fill the available management positions. In this they took suitability rather than seniority into consideration.

Between 1988 and 1991, all first-line managers were subjected to an intensive learning programme. A course was designed along the lines of the action learning model. In this model, practise rules supreme and real-life examples are used as study material. The main objective of the course was to turn the heads of departments into managers capable of directing and controlling their own operations independently. They all underwent the transition from supervisor to manager, to entrepreneur.

Results and evaluation

The delayering process was the result of a change in culture within AEGON. It was a logical consequence of previous, related developments. By giving employees more space, client orientation could be improved.

There are, however, a number of disadvantages to the delayering process. For instance, the pressure on middle management has increased. Heads of departments now have more people reporting to them than before the delayering process. Because the demands on managers have increased, the risk that something goes wrong has grown. Another problem is the fact that the number of managers with integral management skills is limited. Finally, the fact that the scope for promotion has decreased for employees is also considered a disadvantage. A greater effort will have to be made to provide challenges within the individual's job.

Mr Storm has played a pioneering role in leading the change process. Effective 'bottom up' communication ensured that structural changes were received positively. All energy was focused on the middle management, because it was here that new positions were created and a new operational approach was expected of managers.

Not all business units already consist of three management layers, but it is expected that this will be the case in the near future. In the long term, AEGON aims to achieve an organizational structure which is completely orientated towards the business units.

AVÉRO VERZEKERINGEN

This case study describes the restructuring process at Avéro Verzekeringen in which delayering was, and is, one of the themes. This process started in 1990. A combination of external factors – such as increased competition, consumerism and concentration in the financial service sector – and internal factors – such as the desire to improve the capacity to react quickly to market requirements – were the main reasons for the adaptation. In real terms, it came down to turning the organizational structure from a functional one into a structure with a business unit orientation. This involved a large degree of decentralization and market orientation. The number of hierarchical levels in the organization decreased. The delayering process mainly took place at middle management level.

A brief description

Avéro Verzekeringen is part of the AVCB group which came into being through the merger with Centraal Beheer. Within a space of five years, Avéro Verzekeringen itself has, by means of a number of consecutive mergers, developed into a nationally operating insurance group with strong regional positions. Avéro Verzekeringen is involved as intermediary (Avéro Life and Property/Vezeno and Assuring), direct (FBTO, Avéro Pensions, OLM and OVVM) and through the banking business.

The group operates in various insurance markets: property and life assurance and pensions.

Table 3.3 Avéro Verzekeringen business statistics for 1986–1992

	1986	*1987*	*1988*	*1989*[1]	*1990*[1]	*1991*[1]	*1992*
Turnover*	784	862	945	1,214	1,378	1,500	1,600
Profit*	127	106	121	150	142	148	149
Staff		685	763	1,041	1,058	1,130	1,145

[1] Including OLM Verzekeringen en OVVM Verzekeringen
* Amounts in millions of guilders

The old structure

Avéro Verzekeringen used to have a functional, centrally managed structure (see Figure 3.4).

In addition to total co-ordination of the company, top management was mainly concerned with strategic matters. Below the top management, a team of managers looked, each from their own functional responsibilities and supported by their own staff, at the operational processes. The team comprised two managers who had the responsibility for the product groups life assurance and property insurance and pensions. They were responsible for all technical matters (premium conditions, claim settlements, etc.) of Avéro as well as FBTO products. These product groups are organized predominantly by function.

Prior to delayering

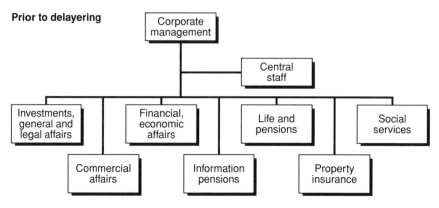

Figure 3.4   Avéro's structure prior to delayering

Reasons for delayering

After a number of mergers and having opted to organize the company structure by function, doubts started to emerge with regard to the general effectiveness of this functional structure for the organization as a whole. These doubts were strengthened by the fact that some of the companies were not integrated because of their regional character but remained independent units. The question was raised whether it would be better if other units were to operate independently and in a result-orientated way. From this point of view, the earlier integration attempt has had a positive effect.

The functional structure led, after a few years, to too large a degree of collective responsibility and long lines of communication (too many hierarchical layers). At the same time, the separation of the various functional layers caused problems of co-ordination and alignment.

In conclusion it can be said that mismatches between external trends and organizational characteristics existed which led to the decision to reorganize.

The new structure

In 1990, Avéro Verzekeringen embarked on the development of a new structure. The most important change was that the organizational structure was turned on its side (see Figure 3.5).

Avéro Verzekeringen's main brands, which were previously located within the functional structure, were moved to independent business units

After delayering

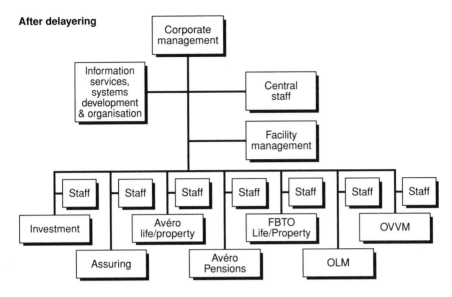

Figure 3.5   Avéro's structure following delayering

with their own product/market/distribution combination. The business units
have the character of a profit centre. The management of the business units
are responsible for their own profits. The business units each have their own
support staff (e.g. Personnel & Organization) or decide to buy in the
services of central staff departments and support services. The latter are
spending departments and their relationship with the business units is one of
supplier and client.

It was not until the third phase of the change process, during the setting up
of the business units, that the matter of delayering came into play. In order
to provide a clear picture of the situation prior to delayering we will briefly
describe the old structure.

The hierarchy in the old organization is displayed in Figure 3.6.

Below the top management came the sector directors of the various
functional groups. Underneath them we found heads of sector groups who
acted as sorts of deputy directors. They were each responsible for several
Avéro or FBTO brand products. Below these came the heads of department
who were responsible for the operational procedures of one particular
product line (e.g. fire and miscellanea in the property insurance division).
The heads of department had a number of teams, each of which was
responsible for a specific part of the functional process (e.g. subscriptions,

complaints or claim settlements) reporting to them. The teams each had a team leader who was responsible for reporting back to the head of department on a regular basis.

In setting up the units within the new structure, consideration was given to the number of layers a unit needed to function effectively. At the Avéro Life Assurance and Property Insurance unit, this led, for Avéro Life, to a total number of three layers (see Figure 3.6). The heads of department and team leaders were replaced by account or product managers. This meant that the layer of divisional manager and head of department disappeared.

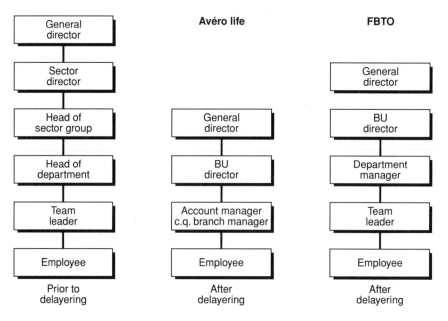

Figure 3.6   Reduction of the number of management layers at Avéro Verzekeringen

The control sphere of the account or product manager and the business unit manager has increased drastically. In some units we therefore find temporary heads of department. In the FTBO unit, four layers remained (see Figure 3.6). This unit has replaced the heads of sector groups and the heads of departments by product and department managers.

Supporting measures

To enable the new structure to function, the following supporting measures have been taken or considered.

By organizing strategic workshops, strategic goals are established in advance and 'shared out' throughout the group. At the end of each quarter, the business unit managers discuss the results of their unit with the top management. Within the business units, the budget is shared out among the accounts managers on the basis of strategic choices and the business plans that were made.

In order to compensate for the growing pressure and the increase in responsibility for results, Avéro Verzekeringen is looking to adapt its reward system but, as yet, has not managed to achieve this. What has taken place is a thorough career interest registration and a selection procedure. Following the selection of the business unit management, an extensive training programme was put into action.

In order to support the decentralization and the increase in control spheres, centralized and decentralized management information systems have been developed and implemented. At the same time a performance information system has been developed so that the top management can quickly detect any variations and correct these in time.

The responsibility for results, the change in operations and leadership all require a change in behaviour. To this purpose, teambuilding sessions were held and an extensive Management Development Programme was started.

The delayering process

The idea that 'things could be done differently and better' had been around for some time, but it was not until the beginning of 1990 that a small group of managers expressed this feeling. An analysis of the company's strengths and weaknesses led to the conclusion that change was inevitable. Agreement between top management and the management team was reached during three management conferences held within the space of a few months. It was decided, in principle, to opt for a rapid change process.

Phase 1: analysis and policy development

In order to radically change the orientation of the entire organization, a restructuring programme was developed, led by a programme manager and supported by a programme bureau. Within this programme, a large number of projects were set up. One of these projects was a full analysis of the operational management of the company (called PPA: Personnel and Process Audit). In addition, an audit of the existing information systems was carried out. In a large number of brainstorming sessions a new market-orientated strategy was defined. At the same time a new top and organization structure containing business units was developed.

During this phase, efforts were made using various means of communication (company bulletin, briefing sessions, gimmicks) to brief middle management and employees. This phase reached its conclusion with the appointment of the new business unit managers.

Phase 2: organizational development

Following the appointment of the business unit managers, the accent of the restructuring programme shifted to the units. Authority and responsibility for results also moved to the new business unit management. During a number of work conferences each unit concentrated on appointing staff at departmental level. After these middle management positions had been filled each unit drew up a new business plan. The new business unit management clarified these plans for their own staff (in so-called 'soap box sessions').

Apart from these activities at unit level, this phase saw the completion of a number of integral projects. These projects were:

- the development of a completely new reporting and policy cycle
- the decentralization of part of the central staff departments
- the realization of the new legal structure
- an extensive training programme for the complete unit management.

This phase was concluded with a celebration of the beginning of the new organization. All units appeared fully equipped at the starting line.

Phase 3: execution – delayering the units' middle management.

Following the actual conclusion of the 'tilting operation' in July 1991, the units took up the implementation of the new management philosophy (delegation and entrepreneurship).

The phasing of this implementation was identical to that of the main programme:

- analysis of the processes and definition of policy
- development of a new structure (tasks and responsibilities at department and account level)
- appointment of new middle management and personnel, and development of the necessary means (training, systems, etc.).

This phase ran from July 1991 to approximately the beginning of 1992.

Evaluation and follow-up

The process took place at high speed, but was, nevertheless, rather successful. A master plan was developed in which a number of steps could be distinguished, but within this plan there was room for improvization.

The follow-up process is still under way, which is why it is rather difficult to assess the effect of the entire operation. In general, the new structure at Avéro Verzekeringen is viewed as positive.

People enjoy working in smaller groups with their own identity and the ensuing increase in responsibility and involvement in results. The responsibility for profits lies with the unit and is not spread out over the various organizational parts. Because of this unity in policy, it is possible to realize projects more rapidly and to take better advantage of developments in the market.

During the entire process, the following dilemmas arose for which a solution had to be (and was) found:

- shortening the lines of communication
- stimulating delegated entrepreneurship
- improving productivity and efficiency
- solving historical problems which had 'dragged on for years'
- stimulating product innovation
- building up an adequate reporting system for management.

In the near future, the following areas will continue to require attention.

Communication and participation

Communication can never be too intensive. Insufficiently informed employees become insecure, obstructive or leave the organization. Participation can lead to a good input as well as feedback. It will equally have a positive effect on the involvement of employees lower down in the organization. 'Management has to be prepared to say where they stand and to explain why something happens'.

Careful appointment of key figures

The appointment of key figures has to be handled with great care. This not only goes for the appointment of people in new positions, but also for the composition of the various project groups. A good representation of line managers is an advantage: after all, they are the people having to implement the changes. At the same time, departments starting to fight over good people should be avoided.

Attention to automation

The development of information systems suitable to the new organization with its new information needs is of major importance. In order to be able to operate in a market-orientated way the rapid processing and translation of information is essential.

Further development of entrepreneurship

Within the business units, and especially at middle management level, the development of responsibility for the company results and an entrepreneurial style of management will require further attention. This will also ensure a better performance with regards to the market.

HOOGOVENS IJMUIDEN

In this case study we look at the organizational development and the corresponding delayering at Hoogovens IJmuiden. Delayering has never been a leading theme at Hoogovens IJmuiden. It was simply a logical consequence of other far-reaching organizational changes, such as the turning over of the production organization. Delayering took place in the Production and Technical Services Department, among others.

A brief overview

Hoogovens IJmuiden (which will be referred to as Hoogovens) is part of Koninklijke Nederlandse Hoogovens and Staalfabrieken (Royal Dutch Blast Furnace and Steel Factories) NV and accounts for 50 per cent of the group's turnover. Hoogovens produces a number of steel products, varying from rolled sheet metal to reinforced and packing steel.

Hoogovens is a unique company with an integrated production chain which consists of linked, capital-intensive, mammoth installations. Building a new blast furnace would require a capital investment of 750 million guilders. An area of almost 2,000 acres offers employment to about 14,000 people and 'harbours' the third largest port of the Netherlands. This makes Hoogovens a company with unique management problems.

Table 3.4   Hoogoven's business statistics from 1989 to 1992

	Hoogovens IJmuiden				Group	
	1992	1991	1990	1989	1992	1991
Turnover*	4,202	4,161	4,205	4,725	7,722	8,095
Profit*	(234)	(98)	230	495	(595)	(51)
No. of employees	14,215	15,269	15,687	16,501	25,593	26,248

* Amounts in millions of guilders

Hoogoven's old structure

Hoogoven's structure, which changed drastically in 1988, was organized centrally by function (see Figure 3.7).

The Production Department consisted of several sectors, each responsible for part of the total production process. For instance, production planning and quality control took place at a central level.

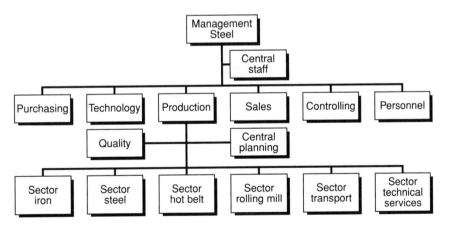

Figure 3.7   Hoogoven's old structure

Reasons for delayering

A combination of external and internal developments made it necessary to introduce a number of change processes. This led, among other things, to a partial delayering of the organization.

External developments

The international steel market has suffered from overcapacity since the late 1970s. During the last decade, a certain amount of rationalization took place. The early 1980s saw production quotas being fixed at a European level. Overcapacity nevertheless remains a problem. Competition has increased enormously. Achieving a cost-leadership position in this market is therefore of vital importance.

Hoogovens competes at an international level against Japanese and Korean steel manufacturers whose productivity is very high. Increasingly, eastern European steel manufacturers are starting to play a role (although their steel tends to be of a lower quality).

Market requirements have furthermore become more important. In addition to quality, delivery periods and variety of products play important roles in the battle for customers.

All these external developments caused enormous pressures on an organization the structure and planning systems of which had largely evolved in the 1960s.

Internal developments

In order to be able to react to the external developments described above, a number of change processes were put into place. We will briefly describe the most important ones. All change processes were brought together in the Master Plan which was implemented at the beginning of 1992 (Figure 3.8).

In Table 3.5 these change processes are outlined.

Improving productivity

The development in costs caused the need for a reorientation. In a large-scale cost study, each part of the company was compared to an ideal model, which was based on data from the best steel plants in the world. This study showed that productivity, measured in man hours per tonne of steel, was, on average, 30 per cent lower at Hoogovens. It was therefore decided that costs

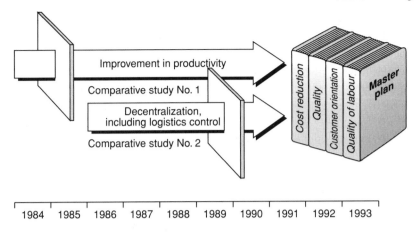

Figure 3.8   The change processes at Hoogevens set against time

Table 3.5 The change processes from 1986 onwards

Plan of action	Dates	Key words	Reasons
Improving productivity	1986	20% in three years	Cost development and comparative study No. 1
Decentralization	1988	Reorientation of product Organization and contract Management	Market requirements and simplification of the physical flows
As part of which: logistics control	1989	Decentralized	Efficiency and time span
Master Plan	1991	Achieve objectives	Comparative study No. 2

should be reduced by 20 per cent over a period of three years, starting in 1986. The development of costs is monitored constantly. One of the objectives of the Master Plan is to reduce costs even further.

Decentralization

In the early 1980s, management at Hoogovens began to realize that the organizational structure was no longer adequate. Control of the centralized, functional organization had become too complex. It became ever more difficult to plan at a central level and to meet market requirements (such as quality, delivery times and product variety).

On the basis of a report by an external consultant, it was decided to appoint a task force. A prerequisite for the realization of a number of proposals from this task force was a change of the organization: from a central, functional organization to a decentralized, integrated organization. In 1987, the decision to decentralize was made (see Figure 3.9).

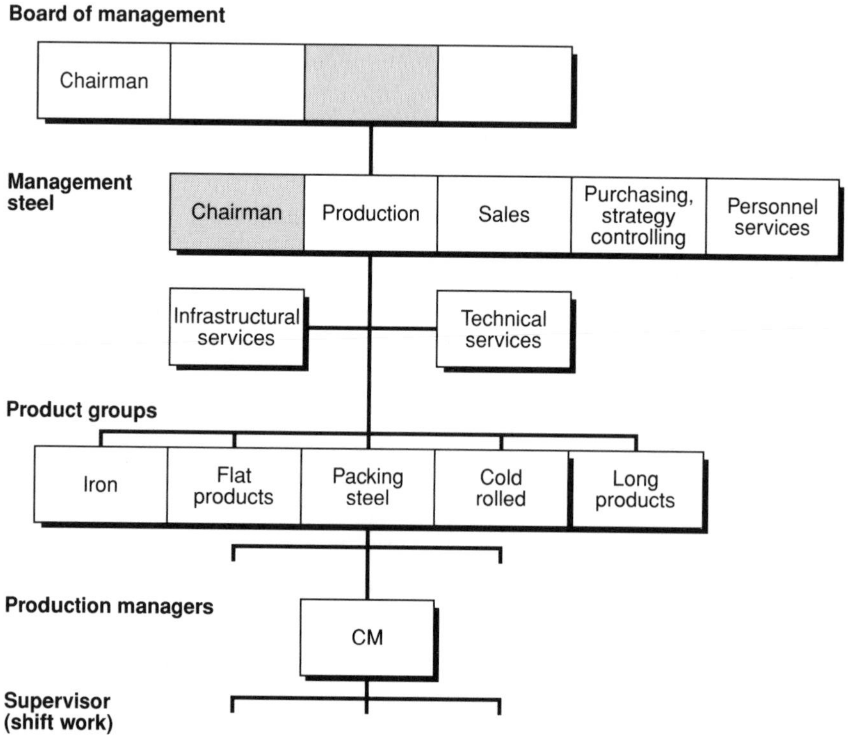

Board of management

Figure 3.9   Hoogovens' new structure

The management philosophy was based on the idea that all of the expensive production equipment was to be used. This meant that other performance indicators, such as time span, customer-order management, etc., were somewhat neglected. Decentralization and adjustment of logistics management have led to a better understanding of inventory, delivery times, etc.

The Master Plan

In 1989, another large-scale comparative study was carried out in which Hoogovens was compared to an equivalent Japanese steel manufacturer. This study formed the basis of the Master Plan with which Hoogovens hopes to achieve the following goals:

- reduction in costs (by reducing the number of contractors)
- improvement in quality
- increase in market orientation
- improvement in the quality of work.

The delayering process

The primary process was clearly process orientated (Figure 3.10). In 1988, within the framework of the decentralization process, the primary process was arranged by product (see Figure 3.11).

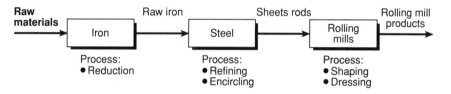

Figure 3.10   From being process-orientated to . . .

We can now see five product units, of which four produce end products for specific markets.

Delayering within the product groups

Within the decentralized units, integral management responsibility has been introduced. The co-ordination point is now located much lower down in the organization. The Production Manager, for instance, now has to meet in person with the Product Group Manager and those responsible for infrastructural and technical services. Prior to decentralization, these matters were discussed at the level above. Now the relationship with the market is more direct and the time needed to make decisions has been reduced.

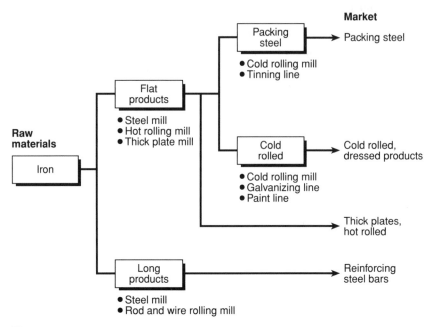

Figure 3.11   Being product-orientated

The total number of management layers within the five product units shows a tendency towards delayering because of a reduction in the number of supervisory functions and the introduction of semi-autonomous task groups. No uniform approach has been devised for this. The management structure can vary from unit to unit, depending on circumstances such as (dis)location of production facilities. In one product group, for instance, the production facilities lie 1.5 miles apart. This creates the need for one manager per facility. In other units, this 'intermediate layer' is not necessary.

Delayering of the Technical Services Department

Prior to the organization's shift in orientation, some 5,000 people were employed by the central Technical Services Department. The Department also hired in a further 2,000 external people. The number of hierarchical layers was seven (see Figure 3.12).

During the decentralization phase some 2,000 people were transferred from the central Technical Services Department to the various units. During

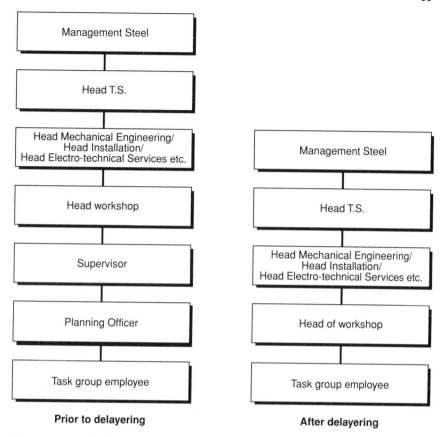

Figure 3.12   Delayering of the Technical Services Department at Hoogovens

the reorientation, a number of tasks, such as controlling, personnel, technical services, and, in some cases, quality, were decentralized. For those parts of the Technical Services Department which will continue to operate from a central level, delayering is the objective of a reorganization process. Reorientating the service departments was intended to reduce the number of 'double access points' for the internal customer. Partly because of the integration of these access points, delayering was made possible. The number of layers in the new structure (Technical Services) has been reduced by two. The layer of supervisory and planning officers has disappeared.

The scope for delayering was mainly realized by reducing the number of people working in the Technical Services Department. This was partly achieved by reorganization. By engaging the various service groups on the basis of tasks and products it became possible to simplify the structure, to operate in a more product-orientated way and to target co-operation more towards results.

The change process

Decentralization and the corresponding delayering involved the following principles:

- task force approach
- time for employees to be debriefed and prepare briefs on their old jobs
- rapid implementation
- give clarification.

The process was managed from the top down, with the appropriate management team playing an important role in the implementation.

Task force approach

A task force was set up to construct a plan for the implementation of improvements in productivity. This task force did, in fact, initiate the reorientation and consisted of people with a wealth of experience and a very broad base.

Allow time to establish, transfer and relinquish

Many of the employees had worked for years within the old structure and had built up a large expertise, but, at the same time, found it difficult to relinquish the old set-up. Those employees who were to be transferred were given time to write their own 'testament'. This meant they could pass on all relevant knowledge and relinquish their old position.

Rapid implementation

The new structure was implemented rapidly because management felt it was important to keep the period of uncertainty to the absolute minimum. Management's role changed in this phase from 'coach' to 'pioneer'. This meant that they sometimes needed to use their powers of persuasion in order to push the changes through quickly. Line managers played an important role in this change process.

Provide clarification

Management also thought it very important that, during the entire process, sufficient clarification was given. The communication took place leapfrog fashion: every manager was expected to inform the two management layers below.

The design and implementation of a thorough communication plan was seen as a sizeable task for management.

In realizing the Master Plan, management employed the following principles to help implement changes:

- employees were asked to participate in policy making
- objectives were set, but not cast in stone.

Participation in policy making

All staff were involved from a very early stage in the change process. As early as the preparation phase, employees were asked to generate ideas and comment on proposals for change. Those in charge explained the objectives. On this basis, proposals for the realization of these objectives were communicated from the bottom up. This process was referred to as 'carolling'.

Objectives were set, but not for ever

The change processes were alterable. Management collectively set out the objectives which the organization, insofar as was possible, was expected to realize. The organizational units were mostly free to decide on *how* to realize them.

Evaluation

At Hoogovens the entire change process followed the evolutionary model. Gradually, and sometimes in leaps and bounds, costs were reduced, productivity was raised and quality improved. Without having to resort to forced redundancies the number of employees was reduced from 22,000 to 16,000 in the 1980s.

By reorientating the production division and reorganizing the Technical Services Department, the following objectives were realized:

- The organization changed from a centrally functionalized one into a decentralized integrated one. By reducing the number of supervisory layers and introducing semi-autonomous task groups, delayering was achieved. The co-ordination point was lowered.

- The Technical Services Department was largely decentralized. At a central level, service groups were introduced with the aim of giving the internal customer one access point.
- The organization has become more transparent. In the new set-up, it is easier to track the relationship between the costs and revenue of the various activities. The centrally organized Technical Service groups have to offer their products at competitive rates, which means that the added value is easier to trace.
- The organization is in better shape. The experience gained enables the organization to react more easily to any changes that are required. Productivity and control have improved while costs have been reduced. The Production and Technical Services Department has seen a reduction in size and number of layers.

A number of issues still have a high priority.

- The production units have to achieve a larger measure of independence. By developing and recruiting managers able to cope with integral responsibility, the units will become less dependent on the support services and able to operate with fewer of the employees which were transferred from the central staff departments.
- The issue of control requires some attention. This does not only concern control of the primary process, but also of decisions regarding decentralization (will issues such as the environment, the issuing of rules and regulations, and safety remain centrally organized or is it possible to organize these at a decentralized level?).
- The support services will have to gain shape. The process which enables the production units to buy in services from the central support services through contract management will have to develop in such a way that it has optimum effect on the organization as a whole. This also raises the question of 'make or buy'; co-production and/or outsourcing.

Conclusion

Following the conclusion of the study, new developments have taken place at Hoogovens. Within the objectives of the Master Plan an additional reduction in costs is required within three years.

DOUGLAS AIRCRAFT COMPANY

In this case we will describe the process of delayering as part of a process of installing a Total Quality Management System (TQMS) at Douglas Aircraft Company. Douglas Aircraft Company (DAC), a part of the St Louis-based McDonnell Douglas Corporation (MDC), has a 70-year tradition of delivering quality aircraft products and services to customers around the world.

After elaborating the reasons for delayering, we will take a look at the structure after delayering; the process of delayering, as well as the features of that process; the new role of the management; and the supportive measures which can be seen as a critical success factor. Finally, we make a short evaluation and look at future perspectives.

Brief overview of DAC and MDC

The DAC was founded in 1920 by Donald W. Douglas and five employees to build the 'Cloudster', a wood and fabric aeroplane that was the first to lift a payload equal to its own weight. Since then DAC has delivered more than 46,500 commercial and military airplanes, and the long line of Douglas Commercial (DC) models have a history of more than 50 years' continuous service world-wide.

In 1967, DAC, the California-based legendary builder of the DC-3 Dakota, merged with McDonnell Aircraft Company, a well-established producer of advanced fighter aircraft in St Louis, Missouri, to form MDC.

Since 1988, John F. McDonnell, jr., son of the founder of the McDonnell Aircraft Company, has been the chairman and CEO of MDC. MDC produces military and commercial aircraft, transport aircraft, space systems and missiles, and provides financial services.

MDC has a wide range of programmes in production and development, and is one of the world's leading producers of military aircraft. Since 1987, MDC has been the largest US defence contractor. In addition to its large volume of defence business, MDC received many contracts from NASA and has also received significant contracts in the commercial space market. MDC is one of the three principal manufacturers of large commercial transport aircraft outside the former Soviet Union.

DAC accounts for 38 per cent of MDC's revenue and, since 1989, has been led by President Robert H. Hood, jr. DAC's primary design, final assembly and testing facilities are located at Long Beach, California. Seven off-site facilities manufacture and assemble component parts and sub-assemblies, which are then shipped to Long Beach for final assembly. In all, 24 facilities with more than 17.4 million square feet provide administration, engineering, production, basic and applied research to support aircraft and associated products. DAC's employment in 1993 for pure commercial activities is 14,993, 22 per cent of MDC's total employment.

Commercial aircraft currently in production at DAC are the wide-body MD-11 long-range tri-jet and the twin-engine MD-80 and MD-90 short-to-medium-range transports. DAC's military programme, the advanced technology C-17 transport for the US Air Force, was transferred to MDC in 1993.

MDC's aerospace segments compete in an industry that consists of a few major competitors and a limited number of customers. The programmes and products that comprise most of MDC's business volume are of a highly technical nature, comparatively few in number, high in unit cost and have traditionally enjoyed relatively long production lives. The branch of aerospace industry can be called cyclical and is very hard to automize, which implies that it is very labour-intensive.

The old structure of DAC (1988)

The organization chart of DAC, prior to the process of delayering, which started in February 1989, had seven layers of management. Including the control structure of MDC and the divisions, there were up to nine layers. DAC used to have a very complex decision loop, with functional support organizations responsible for several different aircraft programmes. The old arrangement required both functional and project officials to approve decisions. The master organization of DAC (1988) is represented in Figure 3.13

An essential feature of the old DAC organization (1988) was the 'silo structure' with great barriers and walls between the functional departments. Operations management and programme management in both commercial and government products were strongly separated. When operational problems had to be tackled from the top, it appeared that people did not even know each other. The management style could be characterized as rather paternalistic and often dictatorial.

Focusing on layers from top to bottom of the operations part of the organization, there were at most times seven layers in the 'layered pancake'.

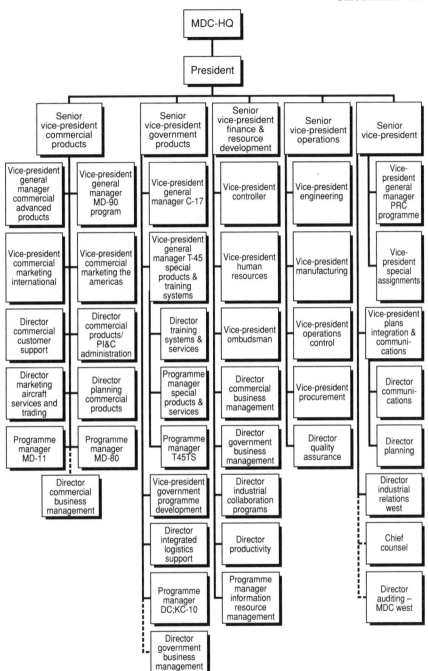

Figure 3.13   Master organization at DAC in 1988 (before delayering)

Reorganization of DAC launched by John McDonnell, jr. in 1989

'Sometimes it is necessary to take a step backward in order to move decisively forward.' Since 1980, MDC has been on a path of changing its management culture. It started with study and observation, then proceeded to formulation, exhortation and experimentation.

In 1989, the phase of implementation was reached and John McDonnell, jr., who became Chairman in early 1988, decided that the entire group needed a radical overhaul of its management systems. He introduced the so-called Total Quality Management System (TQMS); inspired by the Japanese, it had been adopted by several other leading US manufacturers.

DAC became the first part of the Corporation to implement this comprehensive, company-wide TQMS. They started with this part because the need for change and the potential for improvement were the greatest in this business, which had a huge backlog.

At that time, few empirical studies were done on this rather new subject and, because the process of TQMS takes a long time (and never ends), it was difficult to act on the results and feedback of other companies.

Reasons for delayering

Both external and internal developments were forcing the delayering decision in DAC as one of the elements of the implementation of TQMS there. During the period 1970–1982, DAC had enjoyed an exceptional reputation for the quality of her aircraft – best structure, efficient to operate, moderate demand. Besides, deliveries of orders were on schedule and characterized by predictable costs. The organization's focus was control; an approval hierarchy in which functions dominated.

In the following period, from 1983–1989, there were pressures to change. Although DAC's reputation for quality remained, that quality had too often been achieved at too high a cost. The amount of inspection and rework involved meant the company had not earned a satisfactory return on its investment. As a result, DAC ranked near or at the top of the aerospace industry in sales, and near or at the bottom in profit margin.

DAC had to move with the times from a technical and functional approach towards a more product- and service-orientated organization. Its decreased profits might be blamed, in part, on the competitive pressures of the aerospace industry, but was also a result of internal developments – cost problems related to development of new models and model changes, changes in production rates, part problems, overloaded systems, structure and late deliveries.

The management did not have a sufficient grasp on real production costs, while suppliers complained about bureaucracy and inefficiency in the purchasing system. Elementary operational and financial controls were lacking and the traditional 'fix it' approach was too cumbersome for a dynamic market-place.

Accustomed to a rather stable environment, DAC felt the pressures for change from a quickly changing environment, but DAC was hindered by internal factors stemming from a relatively stable success period.

Box 3.1   Pressures to change and background of DAC

Background Douglas 1970–1982	Pressure to change Douglas 1983–1989
Quality aircraft: – best structural integrity – efficient to operate – moderate demand. On schedule Predictable costs Organization's focus: – control – approval hierarchy – functions dominate.	Changing environment: – strong demand – new programmes (MD-11, C-17, T-45) – stronger commercial competition (Boeing, Airbus, BAe) – customer focus. Rising costs Organizational focus: – bureaucratic – overloaded systems and structure – traditional fix-it approach was too cumbersome for a dynamic market-place

'Culturally, MDC was a strongly hierarchal organization of people with a fierce pride – bordering on arrogance – in their technical and engineering excellence. We did not always listen to what the customer had to say before telling him what he wanted.' (John McDonnell, jr., *Annual Report*, 1989).

In the external market environment, there was significant competition in the aerospace industry, both in military and commercial programmes. Two trends can be observed: reduced defence spending through cutbacks in government programmes as well as a decline in the demand for commercial aircraft as a result of the recession; airlines piled up one loss on another, cancelled routes and aircraft orders and squandered the revenues of an increased number of passengers in cut-throat competition.

In the total market, Douglas' position strongly declined; in the last ten years, the market share decreased from 50 to 11 per cent. DAC's opinion on this was that, 'DAC currently designs and markets air-transports for three of six world-wide market segments, competing against the world leader Boeing and Europe's Airbus industry. The MD-80 and MD-90 Douglas twin jets and the MD-11 tri-jet own 35 to 40 per cent of the backlog in their respective market segments. The MD-87, a third, smaller twin jet, holds 7 per cent of its market segment'.

In response to the aforementioned stronger commercial competition, DAC developed many new programmes: MD-11, C-17, T-45. Innovations and constant research and development (R&D) are necessary to remain competitive, but also imply a (financial) risk – interest costs rose enormously.

Moreover, there had been an enormous growth of employees from 1983 to 1989, from 18,000 to 52,000 which, combined with early retirements in the senior ranks, resulted in the experience level of the average worker dropping from ten years to two in that period.

Another way of organizing was necessary; a 'team approach' to setting goals and solving problems depends on breaking down barriers between different functions and disciplines and focusing everyone on the ultimate objective of making the best-quality product for the customer at the lowest possible cost.

Delayering of middle management and TQMS

John McDonnell, jr., introduced in 1989 – as a shock therapy – a delayering at the middle management levels as part of his TQMS. To do this in DAC, he replaced the President and installed as new President Robert J. Hood, jr., the former head of McDonnell's missile systems group which gained a reputation in the industry for high profits and tight cost controls on the assembly line.

'We faced two great challenges: one external and one internal. The external challenge was to produce high-quality, low-cost products that clearly respond to customer needs in a world of rapidly increasing competition. The internal challenge was to continue to develop the kind of corporate environment which enables this to happen by enlisting the full capabilities of our whole team to achieve continuous improvement in all our activities'.

A structural change was needed to shake up DAC. The concept of TQMS was used, because 'the concept is great, conceptually OK, and the operation had to be labelled. TQMS is aimed at tapping the full talents and energy of all our people by stripping away bureaucracy and authocracy and encouraging teamwork and leadership at all levels'.

Key elements were: to crush the silos, bring in new management (style) and create employee involvement, bring significant attitudinal changes in order to reach process orientation and accountability, be competitive again and work for customer satisfaction (both external and internal).

The challenges for the future were clear. Early actions (1989) as elements of the new vision and TQMS approach were as given in Box 3.2.

The new structure of DAC (February 1989)

The new structure (see Figure 3.14) streamlined the company into four product divisions, an extensive Quality division, plus divisions to support business development, product centre operations, commercial marketing and planning and support, and nine divisions or 'vertical business units' in total. This organizational change was influenced by some key factors from the business environment, such as heavy R&D (free new models) and high production rates. The new organization with semi-autonomous product divisions permitted the focus of resources on each product. The new structure reduced levels of management and, hence, was expected to speed up and facilitate communications and decision making. The new leadership team included a core of people from DAC, as well as an implantation of top management from all over MDC, brought in from St Louis.

The number of levels under the old situation of DAC leadership is compared with those under the new situation (February 1989) in Figure 3.15.

Essential was that the new structure had product-orientated management in which each product line – MD-80/DC-9, MD-11/DC-10, C-17 and T-45 – included the support functions necessary to do its job and could be run like a company within a company. The aim was to give each product organization the authority and tools to perform its work, but also to be directly accountable for the results.

In addition, there were three support organizations – Quality division, strategic business and technology development – and the support and plans integration organization.

The Douglas management ranks and organizational structure were changed drastically in February 1989. The seven layers of management were pared down to five. The previous positions of 245 Douglas executives were cut to 80 and the centralized support organizations were broken up and

Box 3.2   TQMS – the vision, approach and actions

People and teams	Disciplined systems	Supportive culture
Restructured organization: – removed layers on positions of management – structured along product lines – horizontal integration New leadership: – new senior team – assessed 5,000 managers – team evaluation and selection Labour management partnership: – joint agreement – UAW parallel structure Employee teams formed: – responsibility, accountability and authority (RAA)	Refocus quality assurance: – quality designed in – measured at all levels – QA steps on design team Process verification and documentation: – continuous improvement – company-wide tracking measurement and reporting – legitimate home for Statistical Process Control (SPC) Root cause problem solving: – training Supplier partnerships: – supplier management function established	Right people for the right jobs: – new hiring orientation – management position selection criteria Empower work force: – RAA – everyone involved Increased job satisfaction: – trust, respect and enrichment Training is emphasized: – training, training, training Open communication: – 'news DAC' – TQMS updates – quality times – leadership meetings

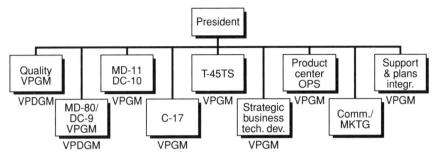

Figure 3.14 Organization chart following implementation of TQMS in February 1989

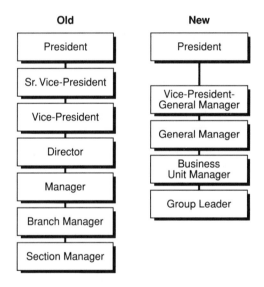

Figure 3.15 DAC's organizational structure: number of layers before and after delayering

made permanent parts of each of the aircraft programmes. The move gave each programme the special resources it needed to do its work.

The 'shock therapy' also included that on 'massacre Monday', February 13, 1989 – every one of Douglas's 5,000 managerial and supervisory positions was eliminated. The former occupants of those jobs could apply for just 2,800 newly created posts. The 2,200 who were to lose out would be stripped of their line managerial responsibilities, but could apply for other lower level jobs. Some left, but many of them were put to work as technical staff specialists on Japanese-style teams, both in design offices and on the production lines.

'Multidisciplined teams were primarily operating at the "business unit" level, one level up from the bottom rung of management . . . The MD-80 programme had about 30 business units with anywhere from 50 to a few hundred multidisciplined members, depending on their mission and location . . . Such teams were much more powerful than employees at the same management level were in the old structure, under which managers had responsibility for only a single discipline.'

The structure of DAC in April 1991

The present organization chart is not the same as the one following the implementation of TQMS in February 1989. A first change in the organization chart was made in April 1991. Essential changes were:

- separation of commercial and military activities under, respectively, Executive VP commercial and Executive VP C-17
- programme co-ordination of all commercial programmes of business units under the Executive VP commercial
- concentration of operations under VPGM operations.

The new structure is shown in Figure 3.16.

The structure of DAC in July 1993

In 1993 a further regrouping step was taken. The most essential changes were:

- military activities are no longer part of DAC
- centralization of co-ordination and decision making on programmes and operations under VPGM Production Programmes.

DAC is now organized as shown in Figure 3.17.

The business unit concept is no longer there. DAC is organized, again, along the functional line to gain advantages of synergy and direct programme and operations decision making and co-ordination. Some critics say that the situation nowadays is the same as it was before the process of delayering. The principal difference, however, is that in the old 1988 organization chart, 'programmes' and 'operations' were separated; now they are co-ordinated by VPGM Production Programmes.

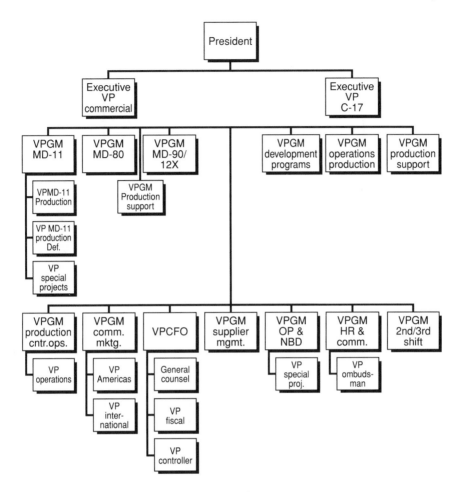

Figure 3.16   Organizational structure of DAC in 1991

Key differences in the business environment compared to 1989 were minimal R&D and low production rates. The result was that the need was felt for clustering functions in a downsized organization to retain and improve efficiency:

'Besides the advantages of synergistic combination of production facilities and moving people around, we have brought management as close as possible to the floor in assembly groups, we realized progress in accountability and through horizontal process orientation and multi-departmental experience; we realized reduced production time, while main-

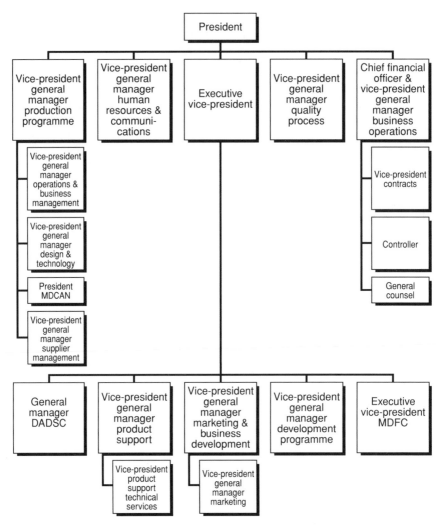

Figure 3.17   Organizational structure of DAC in 1993

taining highest quality at reduced costs. People talk process now. Product is "married" to process and we experience the effects of attitudinal changes we aimed at.'

In the meantime, because of reasons concerning the span of control of management, mainly in production, six layers of management can be found in the organization. Compared with the former situations the layers and titles are now:

President
Vice President/General Manager
Vice President
General Manager
Manager
Group Leader

Features of the delayering and downsizing 1989–1993

Hand in hand with the TQMS implementation at Douglas was the massive downsizing and restructuring of the company, which flattened the organization chart, removed management staff and altered the way aircraft programmes were supported by specialist organizations and by outsourcing of non-core or strategic activities.

The new executive team, drawn from across the company, was despatched to Long Beach, headed by Mr Bob Hood. He started from scratch: departments were reshaped into teams working on individual products, drawing together people from different disciplines. Management layers were cut from seven to five and the new leaders were selected with an emphasis on their ability to 'coach and listen' rather than 'old-style dictatorial management', thus Mr. Hood.

Management layers were cut from seven to five. Supervisory and managerial positions were brought down from 5,000 to 2,800 in 1989 on the day which was called 'massacre Monday'. In 1993 only 1,400 of these positions were left while the number of employees in 1993 came down to 14,993.

There has been a lot of criticism of the way TQM was implemented in DAC. Some critics called it a 'shock therapy'. In the long term, these changes might well prove to be the salvation of Douglas. In the short term however, they produced confusion, demoralization and delays. TQMS was introduced gradually and quite succesfully at MD St Louis division, but was imposed virtually overnight at Long Beach.

According to Mr Hood, jr., the new management team came to Douglas in 1989 with the best plan it could put together. 'There is no textbook on TQM, . . . We assumed there was a level of experience here that would allow us to move rapidly into a full-blown TQMS, and there wasn't. After pushing it down, it didn't work, . . . We had to pull it back to a higher level of experience, work with it at that level and try to slowly move down through the organization. The guy on the floor really wants it.'

Changing market conditions made it like a crisis, '. . . things got worse, before they could get better'. A real turnaround had to be realized. In terms of employment, DAC came down from 52,000 employees (in 1988, incl. C-17) to 14,993 in 1993 in the commercial activities. Besides massive lay-offs in blue-collar, a lay-off of about 10,000 white-collar workers has taken place.

However, since the crisis in 1990, DAC made earning gains for ten quarters and improved its productivity. During the first quarterly period of 1993, $94 million net profit was reported and, since 2.5 years there were no liquidity problems.

The 'anorexia' which took place meant in the meantime that a reduction in personnel took place from 29,000 (1991, incl. C-17) to 14,000 employees. About 10,000 employees were included in the C-17 transfer from DAC to MDC in St Louis.

New role of middle management in DAC

A highly important aspect of the TQMS was the formation of small employee teams on the production line which were to elect their own leader and have the authority to conduct planning, manage their work and make their own decisions rather than waiting for direction from management.

Following the reorganization, the new slate of Douglas executives argued that these employees – more than any others in the company – were in the best position to improve manufacturing efficiency and quality because of their first-hand knowledge of the production process. Douglas managers, in effect, were assumed to realize a supporting role. The primary role of management is to lead, assist, coach, teach, listen and clear away obstacles. It is also a critically important part of a manager's job to ensure that the systems and processes by which work is accomplished support the people on his or her team and that they have the tools, training and resources to do their job right the first time. And not only that. The leader must also see that the team develops precise means of measuring and documenting their progress in accomplishing the tasks that are before them.

However, the concept of 'empowered' teams at the lowest level of the company was redefined relatively early, while TQM techniques such as improved communications, formalized business processes, multidisciplined teams and a greater focus on quality and customer satisfaction remained. Varying reasons can be given for the redefinition of the original self-managed 'natural' work groups on the production line: 'The concept was brought in too rigorously, and perhaps too uniformly; we overestimated the coaching and mentoring role; there was training in the classroom, but in reality up to the production line there was resistance to change; there were situational aspects to redress and we realized that there was the need for additional training.

The main reason was overestimating the effectiveness of initial training; follow-up was needed on the job. Many DAC managers and workers embraced the new concept and the reorganization; others went underground and resisted it, so that there was obstruction at middle management and operational levels . . . A big problem today still is the dictatorial role . . . If we find them, we will remove these klinkers'.

Evaluation and supportive measures

In Box 3.2 the elements of TQMS that create a supportive environment were mentioned. The process of delayering has to be seen as part of a bigger context. It is of major importance that the people of the organization can handle the mentioned changes. The reorganization created the conditions for a 'new' culture.

Therefore, the effectiveness of TQM depends largely on the way it is introduced; preparation, simplicity, sympathy, honesty, credibility, self-confidence and, last but not least, timing and the speed are required.

The transition at DAC has not been easy. Mr Hood noted two distinct areas that DAC clearly did not pay enough attention to: '. . . communication and training . . . We embarked on a communication plan that we thought would cover everything possible. But . . . if we had doubled it, we would still have come up short'.

Regarding training, Mr Hood said, '. . . we underestimated the amount required'. In some cases, workers went through a two-week "Discovery Training" session in an off-site classroom environment only to be frustrated upon their return because other members of the team had not yet been through the programme'. Discovery Training was suspended in mid 1990.

These 'neglected fundamentals' should also have included defining the expectations management had of employees, setting boundaries of authority and establishing formalized work processes instead of relying on 'tribal knowledge', a reference to the more informal systems in place at Douglas prior to the reorganization. Responsibilities have to be defined and managers should not be let too free. Written instructions have to be given and goals and targets set.

In the meantime (1993), the new vision is broken down from strategic business objectives to very specific operational goals. Performance

Box 3.3   Summary of key features 1988–1993

	1989/90
Motives	• Not the best quality, high costs in operation and development, many programmes in development • Lack of interfunctional teamwork
Key programme elements	• 'Shock therapy: – TQMS as label and concept – new structure in business units – delayering
Effects/'new' problems	• Sub-optimization (costs out of control, duplication, increasing inventories, late deliveries) • Reshuffling/reselecting managers in all functions and layers
Conclusions	• Unrealistically high expectations, process disruption, no experience base for the newly installed five layers, lack of work standards, no training process for continuous improvement and process change, limited operational and financial goals and control tools • Everyone was awake, silos were crushed • Readiness for change created through understood linkage of employment and business in real losing employment and market position
Comments	– TQMS was the right concept at the right place at the right time – Business units as an organization concept (together with delayering) was a vehicle for change to shake up the organization and crush down the silos – Through sub-optimization, over expectations, lack of process/operational and financial control, things got worse before they could get better – (Too) much energy was spent in assessment of management – Delayering to five layers under these conditions was a step too far
	1991/92
Motives	• Late deliveries, uncontrolled costs and liquidity problems • Decreasing demand in markets

Box 3.3 continued

Key programme elements	• TQMS • Stronger programme co-ordination • First step to abandon business unit concept • Defining and flowing down goals, responsibilities for all management layers and giving written instruction • Setting quality, operational and financial controls • Downsizing and outsourcing
Effects/'new' problems	• Elementary quality, operational and financial control tools implemented in the management process • Committed and trained managers • Maintaining productivity and improvement while reducing production
Conclusions	• Management process under control • Organization ready to make product and process improvements
Comments	– Internal operations under control – Awareness of key elements in competive position in decreasing market
	1992/1993
Motives	• Improving product and process performance • Improving competitive position and restoring customer confidence and viability
Key programme elements	• TQMS in DAC as a way of life • Process improvement programmes • Centralization programmes and production/operations (realizing synergistic effects on people and facilities/inventories • Accountability and multicriteria performance measurement in time, cost and quality linked to rewards and promotion
Effects/'new' problems	• Strong people and customer focus • Process orientation (process married to results of organization)
Conclusions	• Stronger competitive position • Ready for regaining market share when the recession is over

Box 3.3 continued

Comments	– 'We are on our way; we reached important milestones and are now ready for new demands from the market.'

measurement is directly linked to these specific operational goals, there is systems feedback and corrective action required through the management layers. Bonus and reward systems are linked to non-union management and worker performance. Wages of union employees are based strictly on seniority.

TQM training is of little use if its impact is not measured. DAC added this critical element of comprehensive measurement of results. Each of the operation companies submitted a 75-page report baselining their status relative to the Baldridge criteria. Teams of independent examiners reviewed the reports, made site visits to each company, and provided a formal evaluation to each company.

They intend to repeat this process annually to document the results of improvement plans that each of the companies will be implementing.

Planning is done in a participative setting with a strong top down commitment. Furthermore a committed evolution of the goals is required in terms of building in the effects of the learning curve. Continuous improvement is necessary, for example, in terms of delivery times, costs of getting there in dollars and time, parts out of position/shortages, defect tags.

Improvement has to be there again and again, is quantitatively measured, and workers and managers have to challenge themselves from period to period to higher targets and changing processes to realize this. So, there is now a downward flow of goals and an upward feedback on what is being done. Process improvement ideas are linked in their consequences up to subgoals and goals on company level. *Jetlines Monthly* is the highlights bulletin to help managers communicate with employees: order and production updates are given, plan performance and sales, earnings, cash, inventory, quality, operation unit costs are made explicit in terms of 'better than plan', 'worse than plan' or 'at plan'; facts and figures on dispatch reliability, delivering and hours are communicated. Videos are also used. The message is 'keep committed and focused on goals'.

Through the years of 1991 and 1992, progress became visible in terms of bringing in right management, and behaviour of accountability. Not realizing improvements was regarded as not acceptable. Appeal to pride was referred to down from management layers to the individual worker.

A fair day's work had to be delivered and compensation and promotion were linked to performance.

DAC offers stock options and has an employee stock ownership and savings plan.

DAC is a unionized shop; for the production workers there is a contract up to 1995. In the meantime, the average for years of experience of employees is up to five years again.

Commodities are outsourced and are now bought, preferably, from ISO 9000-qualified suppliers. Cost reductions up to 30 or 40 per cent were possible through outsourcing.

In production, DAC now has team-based work standards that have to be continuously improved by process change. Technical discrepancies are still going down (lowered by 60 per cent over the last two years), production hours were reduced by 30 per cent and are expected to go down by at least another 20 per cent. Behind schedule times are reduced and will be reduced further.

DAC adopted in 1991 the stringent criteria of the US Department of Commerce's Malcolm Baldridge National Quality Award. DAC's overall performance (as perceived by their customers) is measured now by a customer satisfaction index.

Future perspectives

Especially for DAC, the future actions will be aimed at being the premier transport aircraft company. Quality values will be continuously operationalized from the new DAC vision into operational goals. Elements of the DAC vision are, amongst others: customer satisfaction, first time quality, continuous improvement and increased company worth. DAC wants to be the preferred supplier of customers, a desired place to work and reach superior financial performance.

Operational priorities for 1993 were set in terms of further reduction of development cycle time and costs, improvement of configuration management and inventory management.

Mr Hood's 1993 goals were made explicit to the organization. Managers should flow down these goals to all employees, set group goals and link the group's goals to the President's goals for 1993.

Future production programmes include the MD-12X, the MD-XX and the High-Speed Civil Transport. These and other aircraft in various phases of development broaden DAC's production line.

From the outside world of experts, the following statement underlines the direction DAC has chosen:

'Douglas' strategy is to be as little dependent as possible on the timing of the commercial aircraft recovery. As part of this process, it continues to aggressively reduce direct and indirect headcount as well as R&D . . . In addition to significantly reduced labour hours, out of position work is no longer an issue. The company is attempting to maximize RONA and cash flow and reduce inventory. We remain comfortable with our forecast that the company can earn $75–100 million dollars in commercial aircraft profit in 1993 and 1994.'   (Morgan Stanley, April, 1993)

In conclusion

'If any benefit has come from the financial difficulties which the Corporation has experienced in recent years, it has been in concentrating our minds on becoming both a more stringently cost-conscious company and a more fiercely competitive company. It has also concentrated our minds upon the future. Our future is aerospace. We are going to devote our entire effort to becoming the world's pre-eminent team of customer-focused people producing the highest quality aerospace products and services.'
                              (John F. McDonnell, jr., *Annual Report*, 1992)

AKZO

Akzo introduced a new top structure at the beginning of May 1993. The essence of the changes to the top structure is the disappearance of divisional management and staff. This case study describes the reasons for delayering, the new top structure and the way in which this change was arrived at.

Brief description

Akzo was formed in 1969 after the merger between AKU and KZO, two companies in the salt and chemicals industry.

Akzo is a multinational company with offices all over the world. The turnover was 16.9 billion guilders (c. £5.3 billion) and the trading result was 1.16 billion guilders (c. £360 million) in 1991. Akzo employs 70,000 people, of whom more than 22,000 are in the Netherlands. The product range consists of, amongst other things, chemicals, fibres, coatings and healthcare products.

Table 3.6 Akzo's business statistics from 1988 to 1992

	1988	1989	1990	1991	1992
Net turnover*	16,580.5	18,736.2	17,254.6	16,851.2	16,850
Net result*	842.7	954.2	663.0	579.9	646
No. of employees	70,000	73,500	70,500	67,200	62,500

* Amounts in millions of guilders

The old top structure

'A federation of five divisions', that is what the President of the Board of Management, Mr Loudon, called Akzo's old top structure.

Akzo's various activities were accommodated in five separate divisions:

- Fibres and Polymers
- Coatings
- Pharma
- Chemicals
- Salt and Basic Chemicals.

Every division had its own divisional management and its own staff. Above the divisional management was the Board of Management.

The divisions consisted of a cluster of subsidiaries based around a core business. These subsidiaries were often companies taken over by or merged with Akzo. The divisions had always had a large degree of independence. Responsibilities which would normally lie with the Board of Management, such as the responsibility for divisional strategy and structure, and the size and composition of their staff departments, did lie largely with Akzo's divisional management, while obviously requiring consultation with and approval by the Board of Management. As far as their activities were concerned the divisions, with the exception of the Salt and Basic Chemicals and Chemicals divisions, did not have any strong links with each other. The latter two had expertise regarding market approach and process technology which complemented the other's. A simplification of the old structure is shown in Figure 3.18.

Reasons for delayering of the top

The delayering operation can be seen as a continuation of two major change

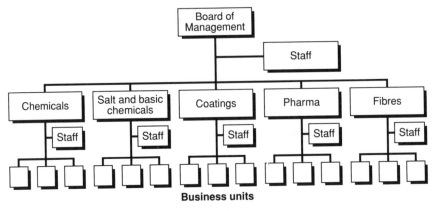

Figure 3.18   Akzo's old organizational structure

processes at Akzo in the last five years: a renewal of corporate identity and the introduction of business units.

At the beginning of 1986, the Board of Management, together with the divisional management, made an analysis of the group's strengths and weaknesses. It was thought that the organization could operate more efficiently. Apart from a number of strengths the following weaknesses were identified:

- the lack of a clear identity
- the policy regarding human resources
- the policy regarding technology
- the synergy between the various parts of the group.

It was decided to tackle first the problem of a clear identity. According to Mr Loudon, this was a real challenge for Akzo.

Akzo was formed through a series of mergers between various companies and this had resulted in an obscure image and the development of an 'island empire'. Many employees felt they were still working for old merger parties such as Sikkens, Organon, Talens or Enka. The differences between the divisions (often one of the merger parties) remained and the exchange of know-how or employees was almost non-existent. The divisions formed sort of autonomous power blocks. This made it rather difficult to manage the organization as a whole and hindered the development of a group synergy.

In addition to the problem caused by the large degree of divisional autonomy and the lack of unity a number of other dysfunctions had developed within the old structure:

- Large staff departments could be found at central and divisional levels and these departments partially overlapped.
- The added value of the divisions had decreased following the introduction of business units because some tasks had moved from divisional to business unit level.
- Communication between the Board of Management and the business units took place via the divisions, so the Board of Management was too far removed from the business units (in some cases divisional Managing Directors were in danger of being bypassed by the business unit management).
- A large amount of bureaucracy was in evidence which led to loss of efficiency and speed and some opportunities not being exploited to the full; staff departments kept each other busy and a large amount of duplication occurred between divisional and corporate level.

The new top structure

The new structure introduced by Akzo is a group structure and was developed in three phases (see Figure 3.19).

In 1989, business units were introduced below the divisional level and the primary entrepreneurial responsibility moved to these units.

Instead of five divisions, each with their own business units, we see, in

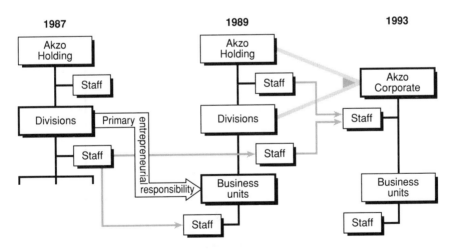

Figure 3.19   Akzo's three reorganizing phases (the figure is an extreme simplification of events and does not take service centres into account)

1993, the emergence of four groups of business units which were brought together on the basis of their mutual synergy:

- Chemicals Group
- Fibres Group
- Coatings Group
- Pharma Group.

The Chemicals Group consists of the merged Chemicals and Salt and Basic Chemicals divisions. The layer of divisional management, including all staff departments, has disappeared. The Board of Management was extended and is now directly in contact with the business units. It is very important to the overall management of the organization that what takes place is management holding, not financial holding. The Board of Management, which is integrated into a Corporate Management Holding, consists, as of 1 May 1993, of six members. Two of these members are only concerned with corporate tasks (the Chairman of the Board of Management and the Vice-Chairman) and the remaining four members have, apart from their corporate responsibilities, responsibility for their own group. Each member of the Board of Management responsible for a group has another Board member as deputy. The Chairman of the Board of Management and the Vice-Chairman obviously fill in for each other in a similar manner. Akzo has thus opted for a so-called 'mixed model'.

Board members with group responsibilities are responsible for the

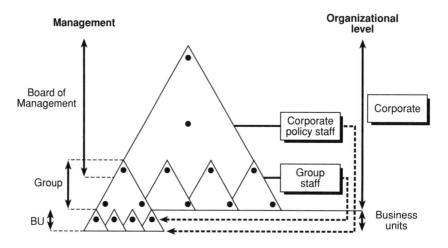

Figure 3.20   Akzo's new corporate levels

objectives of their business unit group being achieved and have the support of a small managerial team which consists, amongst others, of a group director who co-ordinates the technical policy of the business units.

In conclusion the new structure consists of the following concise changes:

- The five divisions have disappeared as organizational entities; they have been replaced by four groups.
- The business units have gained more responsibilities and authority.
- The Board of Management has been extended and now manages the business units directly.
- The staff departments of the Corporate Management Holding company are integrated into four areas; Controlling (ACD), Human Resources (AHR), Finance (AFIN) and Strategic Planning (ASP). Each of these areas has staff employees which are dedicated to a particular group. The recruitment and possible replacement of these staff officers can be vetoed by the member of the Board of Management responsible for the group. The group staff officer manages the staff departments of the business units in their own area (see Figure 3.21).
- Technology is co-ordinated within the groups because a unified organization-wide approach is impossible.
- The reorganization will affect a total of some 1,000 people who are employed in the divisional offices and who will be relocated. In the short term, 200 jobs will be lost and in the longer term some 350.

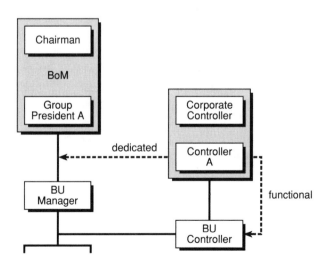

Figure 3.21   Akzo's new corporate policy staff

The most important advantage of the new top structure according to Mr Loudon is the direct communication between the Board of Management and the business units. Information from the units can reach the Board of Management in 'unfiltered form' and this allows it to deal directly with the units. It is thus of vital importance that the members of the Board of Management can give long-term scope to the units.

The process of change and delayering

Mr Loudon has described the process of change and delayering as an 'instinctively created series of inevitabilities'. It was not based on a master plan to change the company culture and structure. The direction in which the process should go was more or less clear and of particular importance was the acquisition of sufficient grass root support for the changes.

The SWOT (strengths, weaknesses, opportunities and threats) analysis found recognition in the Management Council and was validated by them. While it was sometimes difficult to accept immediately the consequences of the analysis at an emotional level, the Council rallied round quite rapidly. The support of the Supervisory Council was also of major importance to the process. The Employees' Council reacted positively to the proposed changes to the structure and enlisted the services of an external management consultancy to independently assess the merits of the new structure.

A decision was made to first of all develop a new identity. When this turned out to be rather successful and received enough support, the momentum and basis were created for the second step: the introduction of business units. Mr Loudon admits, however, that this did require a certain amount of 'missionary work'. The introduction of the business units subsequently led to the new top structure.

Introducing a new corporate identity

In 1986, Akzo started the development of the corporate identity programme. This was, in fact, the first time that internal operations were tackled on an Akzo-wide basis. The implementation of the new identity took place in 1987 with the introduction of the new Akzo logo and the new house style. This was a clear step in the process of becoming one concern with one identity and one culture so that people could feel they were Akzo employees. However, it was never the intention to replace the individual, company-specific cultures.

From 1987 onwards and related to the corporate identity operation, the process of strategy making has changed considerably. After 1987 a single, collective Akzo strategy was developed which then served as a framework for all other activities. A re-evaluation of Akzo's business portfolio was followed by the introduction of units, from which later evolved, more or less spontaneously, the business units.

The introduction of business units

In 1988, Akzo started introducing the business unit concept into the entire organization: Fibres and Polymers (1988/90, followed by Salt and Basic Chemicals/Chemicals (1990/91) and Coatings (1991/92). Within the Pharma division, a business unit structure was already in existence.

The business units were given the authority to make decisions regarding personnel matters, product development, investments and other instruments in order to react to market needs. Business units within groups sharing the same core business were also rearranged: the two chemical divisions were merged into the Chemicals Group.

According to Mr Loudon the business unit concept is often misused. It is by no means the answer to all problems and will not be of value in every situation, but it did work for Akzo. This was because at Akzo it was possible to form units of sufficient size and with their own systems in the area of marketing and product development. Akzo has, however, tailored the concept to suit its own requirements. The autonomy of the business units, for instance, remains within bounds and co-ordination between units is still extremely important. In particular in situations where more than one unit works for the same customer, such as is the case for the automotive industry, co-ordination regarding large accounts is essential.

Introduction of top structure

Following the organization into business units, the changes to the top structure seemed a logical consequence. This certainly did speed up the pace at which changes were taking place. At a meeting of the Management Council in 1991 the Board of Management first made the suggestion that the divisional layer might be abolished. An important factor in this decision was the increased productivity of the business units and the fact that the added value of the divisions and the corporate holding was called into question.

The introduction of a new top structure was seen as a new and exciting step in the change process, and people were particularly keen to see it succeed. The most important management instrument to make the new structure work is the planning and control cycle in which the corporate management and the business units will have to agree on new parameters for a number of areas.

Evaluation

Looking both backwards and forwards, Mr Loudon characterizes the complete change process as 'the search for new equilibriums'. Without the process being directed from a comprehensive plan, the Board of Management has managed to create conditions in which all parts of the group can operate successfully.

During the operation, Mr Loudon adhered to the following principles:

- make sure that there is a large enough basis for any plans, within the Supervisory Council as well as within the organization at large
- do not force changes upon people, but do keep the pressure on them to change
- do look at your top level and make sure that there is agreement of opinion within the Board of Management
- as soon as possible, create clarity regarding the new management direction
- ensure that the 'checking factory' concept whereby individuals mutually and repetitively check each other, is abolished.

The objectives achieved

The introduction of the new top structure was completed in early 1993. This means that Akzo has gained half a year on the implementation schedule. While the entire process has taken almost five years, the last part in particular has been achieved at a greater speed than expected.

Communication and decision making are decidedly faster than before. The business units can deal directly with the Board of Management. A large number of matters can even be dealt with by a Board Committee, i.e., by two Board members with group responsibilities, and the complete Board of Management meets every two weeks. It is possible to get a full picture every month, on the basis of a number of concrete parameters, of the results of the business units which can themselves be discussed quarterly with those responsible – unless, of course, there is a need for immediate action.

The new focus points

At this moment, there are no specific plans for any follow-up. Mr Loudon does indicate that reinforcing relations and synergy within the group will remain the guiding principle for any future changes. Employee participation and corporate identity are two further matters which will continue to receive attention.

There are, however, a number of issues which are of vital importance to the proper functioning of the new structure and which require further elaboration. In addition to the specific control tools, Akzo is, for example, looking to develop and improve (non-financial) critical success factors. Attention is also needed to avoid the old divisional influences and controls sneaking in again through the back door which could affect the idea of profit responsibility at its roots. This means that, apart from a change in attitude, the Corporate Management Holding Company also requires a new style of management, i.e., a more conceptual and stimulating style. At the same time, accountability needs to be a clear starting point and to be based on honest and precise agreements regarding that for which one is accountable. Human Resources, furthermore, requires continuous attention.

The first task of any business unit is to be market- and customer-orientated. Of course, there is a certain responsibility for costs, but this should not lead to endless discussions with the service units. Akzo refers to this as 'squeezing the sausage': there is a limit and insisting on a further reduction in costs will only result in these costs popping up elsewhere. The primary objective, in line with the business unit's market and customer orientation, should be to increase revenue.

Finally, the future will show whether the new managerial teams will function properly and whether their mutual consultation will go smoothly. While the structure of the line management forms a concrete and concise entity, the co-ordination of the various authorities and responsibilities will require further development.

GENERAL ELECTRIC COMPANY

In this case we will describe the process of delayering that took place at General Electric in the 1980s and which continued into the 1990s.

First, we will take a look at GE's organizational structure in 1981, at the start of the delayering process. We will then describe the onset of the reorganization in 1981 and the development of the delayering process, including the organization structure in 1992.

Brief outline of GE's characteristics

In October 1878, Thomas Alva Edison (inventor of the lightbulb) created, together with his friend Grosvenor P. Lowrey, the Edison Electric Light Company. Later on, in 1892, they merged with Thompson-Houston and called the new company the General Electric Company (further on referred to as GE).

GE's original business was in electric lighting and electric motors. Over the years, GE grew into one of the largest and most diversified industrial corporations in the world. According to the rankings in Forbes,[1] based on a combination of its revenues, profits, market value and assets, GE is the world's most powerful corporation,

GE's business portfolio (consisting of 12 businesses) falls into three broad categories:

- *Services* Financial Services, Information Services, NBC
- *Technology* Aircraft Engines, Medical Systems, Plastics
- *Core Manufacturing* Appliances, Electrical Distribution & Control, Industrial & Power Systems, Lighting, Motors, Transportation Systems.

Until the late 1970s GE was only involved in the domestic market. Nevertheless, in 1993, GE was no longer simply a US company. Operating in over 50 countries, in partnerships with many non-US corporations, GE earned over 28 per cent of its operating profits abroad.

GE's market share rose from three businesses (Lighting, Motors, and Power Systems) in 1981 with market leadership, then continued until all 12 businesses had become leaders in their markets in 1992.

Since 1981, John F. Welch, jr., is the Chairman and CEO of GE. GE's Corporate Headquarters are located in Fairfield, Connecticut.

The old structure

In 1968, a McKinsey study led to the creation of GE's Strategic Business Unit structure and the implementation of strategic planning for GE's component businesses. Problems occurred because the SBUs created an imbalance at the top. Corporate management was physically unable to control all 43 SBUs. There was, furthermore a growing concern about the lack of integration and synergy between the many SBUs.

---

[1] In Forbes, 'Forbes International 500', 20 July 1992.

Table 3.6 Financial and employee data of GE since 1980

Year	Revenue ($m)	Net income ($m)	Total employed
1980	24,959.0	1,514.0	402,000
1981	27,240.0	1,652.0	404,000
1982	26,500.0	1,817.0	367,000
1983	26,797.0	2,024.0	340,000
1984	27,947.0	2,280.0	330,000
1985	32,624.0	2,277.0	299,000
1986	42,013.0*	2,492.0	373,000
1987	48,158.0	2,915.0	322,000
1988	50,089.0	3,386.0	298,000
1989	54,574.0	3,939.0	292,000
1990	58,414.0	4,303.0	298,000
1991	60,236.0	4,435.0	284,000
1992	62,202.0	4,725.0	268,000

* Acquisition of RCA, owner of NBC

This led Mr Jones (CEO between 1972 and 1981) to create, in 1977, a *new* layer – *the Sector* – to reduce pressure and improve strategic review, business development and synergy between the SBUs.

The sophistication of the new planning system was reinforced by the quality of staff support. Each layer in the hierarchy had its own staff functions, according to the services it provided to the lower levels. At a central level, the planning structure was supported by a number of boards and committees in addition to the corporate staff.

In 1981, GE was structured into departments (businesses), divisions, groups and sectors. Six sectors reported to the corporate management, and the hierarchy cascaded down from there to 181 departmental general managers. Superimposed on this structure was a strategic planning structure which distinguished three strategic levels: corporate, sector and SBU. An SBU could be a department, division or group as shown in Figure 3.22. In that period nine layers of management were separating the people on the shop floor from the CEO.

In 1981, it was clear that the planning hierarchy, the weight of corporate- and sector-level staffs and the layering of decision-making boards and committees all exerted too much planning influence on the corporate management.

This resulted in an overwhelming bureaucracy and caused a good deal of tension between corporate management and the lower levels, adversely affecting their motivation.

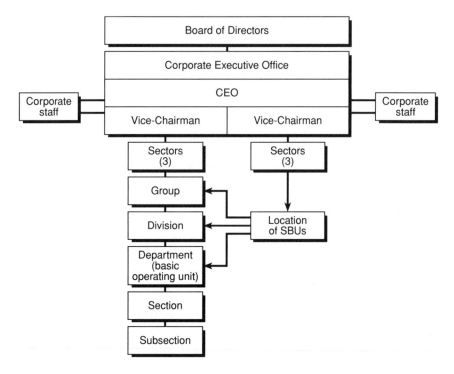

Figure 3.22   GE's organizational structure in 1981

Reorganization launched by Jack Welch in 1981

On 1 April 1981, John F. Welch, jr., became General Electric's eighth Chairman and CEO.

At the beginning of the 1980s, the entire market-place was changing at a much faster pace than in the 1970s: high-tech industries and global competitors were sprouting up. Moreover, higher quality products and new standards of productivity were emerging. Jack Welch was the first head of a major US corporation to realize what impact these changes would have on his company. He was also the first to develop a carefully defined plan to deal with the changes.

While others were saying that GE was in good shape, Welch recognized what most business leaders recognized only later about their companies: that to stay alive and to prosper, General Electric required major restructuring.

Mr Welch had good reasons to think about restructuring. The four reasons listed below all relate to GE's position in the market.

- In 1981, a number of measures pointed to GE's not so favourable competitive position. Only 70 per cent of GE's 350 businesses and product lines were No. 1 or No. 2 in their markets, among them Lighting, Power Systems, and Motors. Of GE's major businesses only Plastics, Gas Turbines, and Aircraft Engines were strong overseas, and only Gas Turbines could claim world-wide market leadership.
- GE's productivity was growing too slowly; it had to speed up the shift from electromechanical to electronic technology; and it needed strong responses to international competition.
- Too many of GE's profits (nearly 50 per cent in 1980) came from product lines which were mature. In a few areas, notably jet engines and plastics, GE was producing leading-edge products, but most of the company's sales still depended on machine-age technology.
- In 1981, GE was coasting on massive backlogs of orders (nearly one-third of annual revenues). Customers had placed most of those orders during the 1970s, long before business conditions changed.

Mr Welch began his reorganization by restructuring the portfolio of businesses (350 in all, clustered in 43 SBUs). He developed a new central focus at GE: the company would only keep businesses that were No. 1 or No. 2 in their markets. Otherwise, the executives had to 'fix, close, or sell' their businesses that did not meet this standard. This was a long-term strategy: GE would readily invest in weak units if they showed sufficient promise of *becoming* strong.

Mr Welch's revolution was formed around a new principle: nothing was sacred. The company had to stop looking inwards. It had to step out into the world, and that meant shedding businesses and managers and employees that were not producing; it meant bringing in new businesses and new managers and new employees that could produce. This was the essence of the restructuring process.

Lay-offs alone could not produce the productivity gains GE needed; the company was also investing billions of dollars in efficient new equipment. Nevertheless, by the end of 1982, the restructuring had already squeezed out 35,000 employees by selling business and product lines, attrition and/or lay-offs, almost 9 per cent of the 1980 total.

The most important divestitures were the sale of Utah International, Family Financial Services, and the Housewares business. The biggest acquisitions were the investment bank Kidder Peabody; Employers

Reinsurance Corp., and RCA, the owner of NBC (in 1986).

Besides the No. 1 or No. 2 rule, the businesses had to be in a high-growth industry, and in the early 1980s that meant either high-tech or services, not the traditional manufacturing businesses.

Reasons for delayering

A restructuring of the business portfolio (including such measures as layoffs, etc.) was not enough for Mr Welch. He knew that he had to change GE's crowded top-heavy structure, which had 29 pay grades, 12 layers of management, and 600 profit and loss units.

GE was left with a couple of internal problems which, together with the external problems listed earlier, gave rise to the delayering process at GE. The internal problems were as follows.

- The wasteful bureaucracy that slowed GE's revenue growth. GE's executives knew how to follow the company's rigid rules but when the outside world began to change, many of GE's procedures and systems became irrelevant.
- The strategic planning system no longer worked in the 1980s. It slowed things down. Managers were not quick enough to spot trouble. Planners wrote memos read only by other planners.
- General Electric had grown so immense and so diverse that nearly everyone seemed to be a manager of some sort. Of GE's 400,000 employees, 25,000 had the title of manager. Some 500 of these managers were senior managers, and 130 were vice-presidents or higher.
- When Mr Borch (CEO from 1968–1972) and Mr Jones reclustered the business units into 43 Strategic Business Units, the command-and-control function was supposed to improve dramatically. But the addition of a new layer of finance and planning staffs resulted in a situation in which executives commanded and controlled one another, leaving them with no time to determine how a business was performing.
- Many of GE's best managers devoted far more energy to internal matters than to their customers' needs. As it was sometimes expressed within GE, here was a company that operated 'with its face to the CEO and its ass to the customer'.

Mr Welch understood that GE faced both an external and an internal challenge. Externally, it faced a world economy with much stronger global competition. To cope with this challenge, Welch had to improve the company which formed the internal challenge.

Mr Welch came up with the *big company/small company hybrid*. It combines a large corporation's resources and reach with a small company's simplicity and flexibility.

Small companies have a number of advantages, which became an important reason for Mr Welch to 'delayer' GE's structure:

- people communicate better, with simple, straightforward, passionate arguments, rather than jargon-filled memos
- small companies move faster: they have to face the reality of the market every day, and when they move, they have to move with speed
- because they have fewer management layers, the leaders show up very clearly on the screen, their performance and its impact are clear to everyone
- small companies waste less, they spend less time in endless reviews and approvals, they have fewer people, therefore they only do the important things.

Mr Welch argued continuously that the key to business success was empowerment of the individual, whether he or she was a middle-level manager or at shop floor level, and the only way these individuals could be liberated was to peel away layers of management. Some said that getting rid of these levels reduced GE's needed command and control and harmed the company. Welch disagreed.

Process of delayering

The CEO had a dual purpose with his 'delayering' of General Electric:

- to turn the strategic planning function over to the businesses
- to remove the obstacles that prevented direct contact between the businesses and between the businesses and the CEO's office.

When Mr Welch took over as CEO in April 1981, he found that three layers of bureaucracy were sandwiched between him and the businesses. Business leaders reported to 12 group executives, who in turn reported to six sector executives, who reported finally to the CEO's two vice-chairmen.

As a first step in the delayering process of General Electric, Welch got rid of the sector bureaucracy. Business leaders today report directly to the CEO.

Another radical change in Welch's first years was the dismantling of a good deal of the strategic planning staff: GE first froze its budget, then eliminated 80 per cent of its jobs. Now GE's operating executives had responsibility for their own strategic planning and were also accountable for their successes and failures.

By the end of 1982, GE had virtually abolished the central strategic planning staff. The logical next step was clearing the sectors (the layer of executive vice-presidents) out of the way, to permit direct interactions with the business heads.

To make sure the sector elimination was the appropriate next phase in GE's delayering process, the CEO urged the executive management staff to study GE's organization. They recommended eliminating the sectors on the basis of the data they collected, and in the context of a whole programme of delicately interrelated structural changes. The basic theme of their argument applies to almost any company: eliminating layers increases an organization's responsiveness to leadership.

These were the motives that were in force for the sector delayering at GE in 1985:

- the sectors slowed down communications and reduced the integration (synergy) of GE's businesses; they allowed bureacratic ways to continue
- the people running the sectors had no power: their role was transmitting information, so they acted as filters, they were in-betweeners, with no way of actually knowing anything first hand
- the main reason for the creation of the sectors in 1977 was a revision of the strategic planning process and, as Mr Welch had already shifted responsibility for strategic planning back to GE's operating managers in 1981, the sectors automatically became unnecessary.

With the abolition of the sector executive layer in December 1985, a shakeout soon followed. Eight months after eliminating the sectors, and one month after closing the RCA purchase (the biggest non-oil acquisition to date, namely $6.3 billion in cash), GE parted company with the heads of three businesses. These events helped trigger a broader reshuffling of top management: by the end of 1986, GE had placed new leaders in roughly two-thirds of its main businesses.

In that same period, the CEO discovered that getting rid of the sectors was not enough, Mr Welch needed something to replace them. Though troublesome, the sectors had helped bind GE together, encouraging a measure of unity among the corporation's otherwise independent operating units. Though the new structure shortened the lines of authority, it was every bit as hierarchical as the old sector organization.

Mr Welch's solution, in 1986, was to create the Corporate Executive

Council (CEC) – a group of GE's 30 highest-ranking business chiefs and senior staff, that meets quarterly to discuss the most important issues facing GE at that time. The CEC is also a device for communication among GE's top leaders concerning the sharing of best practices and the forming of strategies.

In addition to the delayering of the top, GE had also instituted major delayering and streamlining in almost all of their businesses. The CEC concept has permeated down as well. For example, each of the businesses has created its own executive committee which meets to discuss policy questions. These committees meet on a weekly or monthly basis and include top staff and line people from the businesses.

The new structure

Soon after the sectors were eliminated, the gains of the new situation, where the businesses directly report to the CEO, became clear:

- far fewer time-consuming requests for information
- less time spent in the formal review process
- much faster decisions
- quicker, clearer communication.

Nowadays, the corporate head office in Fairfield maintains direct links with business operations and the technology they are developing. In fact, in 1991, Mr Welch ordered all 13 businesses to report simultaneously to him and his Vice-Chairman of that time, Edward Hood (now Paolo Fresco).

Delayering and drastic cuts eliminated the bureaucratic infrastructure that used to prop people up. This has forced GE employees to better understand their businesses, instead of delegating this responsibility to strategic planners or subordinates. And GE executives can no longer avoid tough decisions about what is important enough to spend time on. Once they directly supervised an average of seven people each; now they typically oversee 15 to 20 and sometimes more.

With the delayering process and the redefinition of GE's hundreds of business units in the early 1980s into the present 12 businesses, there are fewer managers with P&L responsibility now: in 1980 there were some 300; by 1992 there were fewer than 50. Businesses also consolidated their staff, increasing the responsibility of functional jobs, but also reducing their number.

Another consequence of GE's delayering process is the authority of

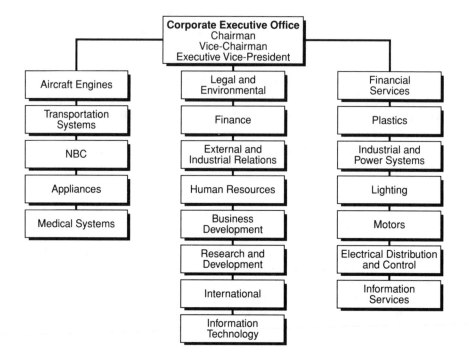

Figure 3.23   The new structure

business leaders over capital allocation. Previously, no executive below sector level could approve a major capital investment without going to the CEO. Now business chiefs have the same authority to approve investment as the CEO.

Supporting measures

Over the years, Mr Welch had driven the organization forwards with an expanding set of slogans, such as 'ownership', with the objective to delegate more decisions and drive the ability to act down several layers; 'entrepreneurship', which meant the creation of an atmosphere in which ideas from all levels could surface; 'reality', 'integrated diversity', and many more.

From the start in 1981, Mr Welch had used the Management Development Institute at Crotonville, New York, to foster cultural change in GE. By

1988, GE's top-level executives understood Welch's ideas, and embraced them (e.g., leaders *owned* their businesses). Nevertheless, Crotonville received a great many complaints about managers further down in the organization. Middle- and lower-level managers still did not see any urgent need to change. Although Welch's ideas were now clear, his communication methods were not effective enough to change people's minds.

The method to further revolutionize GE is called *Work-Out*. This ten-year programme, designed in 1988, began as a series of ongoing, company-wide town meetings, where employees at all levels are encouraged to contribute ideas on how to make GE more competitive.

Today, Work-Out has progressed to become less formal, but more frequent, sessions where bureaucracy is continuously challenged and new ideas are adopted. Other programme elements currently underway to improve GE's competitive position are:

- speeding product development, market penetration and customer service by reducing complexity
- shortening time between order and remittance
- extending stock options to more employees
- courting, inspiring and empowering middle management.

Each of GE's operating businesses now has its own version of the CEC, enabling every business leader to play the 'Welch role'. By mid 1992, over 200,000 GE employees, well over two thirds of the workforce, had experienced Work-Out.

One of Mr Welch's purposes in the delayering process was to improve the synergy among the businesses. Besides the Work-Out programme and the role of the CEC, one of the great sources of synergy at GE was, and is still, the Research and Development Center in Schenectady. For example, highly sophisticated machining and coating techniques designed for the Aircraft Engines business ended up in Power Generation as well.

Evaluation and future perspectives

What we can see, after more than ten years of delayering, is the reduction in the number of headquarters, employees in Fairfield from 1,700 in 1981 to only 400 in 1992. This placed new responsibility on the people who remained. Because they were far fewer, they no longer could do everything that they had been doing. For Mr Welch, this was a positive development.

In a speech to the Annual Meeting of GE's shareholders in April 1988, Mr Welch said:

'They have to set priorities. The less important tasks have to be left undone. Trying to do the same number of tasks with fewer people would be the antithesis of what we set out to achieve: a faster, more focused, more purposeful company. As we became leaner, we found ourselves communicating better, with fewer interpreters and fewer filters. We found that with fewer layers we had wider spans of management. We weren't managing better. We were managing less, and that was better.'

As we can see in Figure 3.24, the entire delayering process within the complete reorganization process has taken a very favourable turn throughout the years.

At GE, productivity growth is believed to be the ultimate corporate weapon for competitiveness. To sustain productivity gains after the restructuring of the 1980s, GE was attempting to tap the human element of creativity and productivity through Work-Out. Traditionally, the managers had the reponsibility for improving productivity. That has now become the task of the men and women on the factory floors.

The company's annual productivity rate has risen from less than 2 per cent in 1981 to a peak of some 6 per cent in 1989, roughly equal to GE's direct

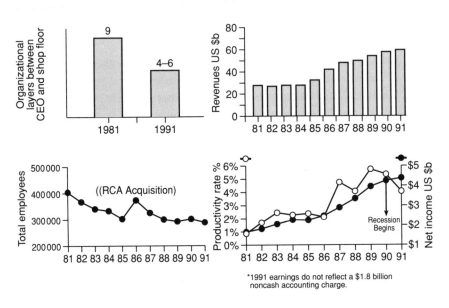

*1991 earnings do not reflect a $1.8 billion noncash accounting charge.

Figure 3.24   Total employees, organizational layers between CEO and shop floor, revenues and productivity

competitors in Japan and only a couple of percentage points shy of Japan's overall rate. Even during the recession, GE achieved 4.5 per cent in 1992.

Over the years, one of the biggest lessons Mr Welch has learned is that change has no constituency and will be met by massive resistance. Incremental change does not work very well in the type of transformation GE has gone through. If the change is not big enough, the bureaucracy will overcome it. Furthermore, in order to promote the 'soft' values, a hardness must first be exhibited. After stripping away the support systems of staff and layers, people need to change their habits and expectations or else the stress will overwhelm them. To create change, direct, personal two-way communication is what seems to make the difference.

For the future, Mr Welch wrote in the *Annual Report*, 1992, 'We are still relentlessly trying to get that small-company *soul*, and small-company *speed*, inside our big-company body'.

ELSEVIER

As we mentioned earlier, the change operation at Elsevier took the form of delayering *avant la lettre*, and went completely against all current trends. In contrast to the majority of organizations which introduced a divisional structure in the early 1980s, Elsevier actually abolished its divisional layer in 1982. Because this operation took place 11 years ago, this is the only case study where we can see the long-term results of delayering. The description of the Elsevier case, therefore, varies from all the others in that we will concentrate on these results.

Brief description

In 1979, Elsevier-NDU was formed out of the merger between Elsevier and the NDU (Dutch Daily Newspaper Union). The activities of the group ranged from the publication of daily newspapers and scientific magazines to setting up courses. The company is active in several markets with a varied product range. In Table 3.7, Elsevier's business statistics of 1992 and of the period around the delayering process (1981–1983) are shown.

As a result of its impending merger with Reed, the concern is one of the ten largest publishing houses in the world. In 1992 the Reed-Elsevier combination achieved a turnover of almost 8 billion guilders (£3 billion). In the same year, their joint profits before tax reached 1.4 billion guilders (£500 million). They employ a total of 25,000 employees.

Table 3.7 Elsevier's business statistics (1981–1983 and 1992)

	1981	*1982*	*1983*	*1992*
Turnover*	1,333	1,292	1,325	2,435
Pre-tax profits*	37	42	53	434
No. of employees	7,589	7,206	7,088	7,440

* Amounts in millions of guilders

The organizational structure prior to delayering

In 1977, two years prior to the merger with NDU, Elsevier introduced a new organizational structure. The main reasoning behind the introduction of this divisional structure was the idea that it would help shape up the expansion policy. Similar to Elsevier, NDU was also organized into a divisional structure.

Figure 3.25 reflects the organizational structure as it was one year after the merger (in 1980). This is the divisional structure of Elsevier-NDU prior to the delayering operation.

At the top of the administrative organization is the Board of Management with its own corporate staff. Underneath the Board of Management we find the following divisions, each with their own management and staff:

- Magazines
- Daily Newspapers

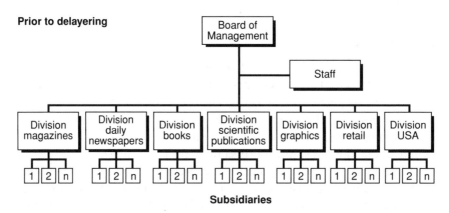

Figure 3.25   Divisional structure of Elsevier-NDU prior to delayering (1980)

- Books
- Scientific Publications
- Graphics Enterprises
- Retail
- United States.

Below the divisional level are the subsidiaries, also each with their own management and staff.

Because of the large number of staff and the extensive layering, the company was fairly 'Byzantine' in character.

Reasons for delayering

A combination of external and, more importantly, internal developments were the impetus for delayering at Elsevier.

Market development

The most important external development which has influenced the Elsevier-NDU organization and relates to the changes in the organizational structure of 1982 is the market development.

Between 1978 and 1981 the markets within which Elsevier operated were still growing. The relatively costly divisional structure was introduced to be able to profit from this growth and by means of decentralized authority react more quickly to market developments. In the early 1980s, the market situation became less favourable and it was necessary for Elsevier to operate in a more competitive way. The Board of Management realized that organizational changes were required in order to be able to achieve this.

Internal developments

In the early 1980s, Elsevier decided to revisit its strategy and set out a number of objectives for the period 1982–1985. These objective were:

- strengthening the profitable activities
- reorganization of those activities that are structurally unprofitable
- savings on costs
- building up a substantial liquidity.

Studying these objectives led to the conclusion that there was a lack of earning power. Elsevier thought that this was due to the following.

- *A lack of competitiveness* The Board of Management was too far removed from the operational reality and its power did not reach as far as the 'front'. The recession required a more direct approach which was hampered by the divisional layer. According to the Chairman of the Board of Management, Mr Vinken, 'The organization did have a steering wheel but with relatively little effect on the direction of the wheels'. Shorter lines of communication, more direct communication and a faster and improved decision-making process were therefore necessary.

- *Insufficient added value* The divisions had expanded enormously during their short life span. The divisional staff regularly collided with the corporate staff. The divisional layer had turned into a type of 'parliament' which made the organization difficult to manage.
- *Overspending* It was thought that costs were not well controlled within the organization. This resulted in a large-scale investigation of costs.

The organizational structure after delayering

During the delayering process of Elsevier's top and the reorganization of the concern, Mr Vinken adhered to the following seven golden rules:

- keep the organization flat
- ensure that there is unity within the Board of Management
- appoint a strong Chairman
- create strong staff, not because of their number, but the quality of the employees
- have staff report directly to the Chairman
- place the final responsibility for strategy with the Chairman
- ensure that members of the Board of Management are managers with 'front experience'.

From 1982 onwards, the management of the subsidiaries reported directly to the Board of Management. To compensate for this, the corporate staff were strengthened slightly by transferring part of the then defunct divisional staff. Furthermore, two former divisional directors were incorporated into the Board of Management. The implementation of this new structure took place at the beginning of 1982.

The subsidiaries were organized into six activity sectors. The word 'sector' was simply an abstract term used to indicate a group of similar activities. There was no formal relationship between the individual sectors. Each activity sector had its own member on the Board of Management to which the subsidiaries reported directly.

The activity sectors which were created were, and still are:

- Trade Information
- Daily Newspapers
- Scientific Information
- Graphics industry
- Public Information
- United States.

The new group structure can be seen in Figure 3.26.

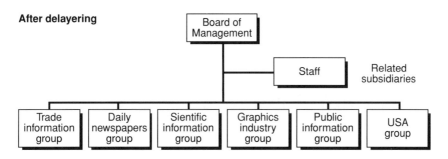

Figure 3.26   Structure of Elsevier-NDU after delayering

Each member of the Board of Management, with the exception of the Chairman who looked after the corporate interests, was made responsible for the results of the activities of one particular sector.

An important aspect of these changes was that members of the Board of Management were now also made responsible for the profit of their portfolio, which guaranteed their involvement.

The corporate staff were reinforced by some high-quality recruitings (at Board level). In addition, they now report directly to the Chairman of the Board of Management. The role of the corporate staff became twofold. On the one hand, it became the 'pilot' which could be 'asked aboard' by the management of the subsidiaries; on the other hand, 'the harbour authorities' could insist that a 'ship took the pilot aboard'.

The organization of the top structure before and after delayering is reflected in Figure 3.27.

Activities which relate to the delayering process

Because the delayering process took place over a decade ago, we will restrict ourselves to discussing only the most important activities. When considering

Prior to delayering

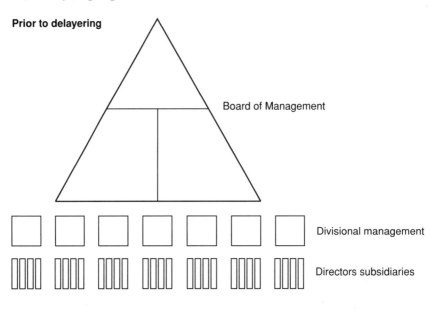

Board of Management

Divisional management

Directors subsidiaries

After delayering

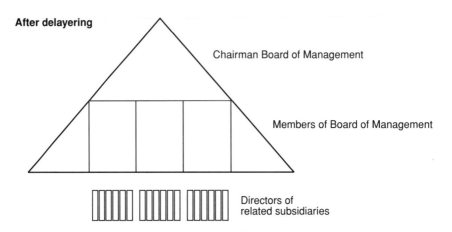

Chairman Board of Management

Members of Board of Management

Directors of
related subsidiaries

Figure 3.27   Elsevier-NDU's top structure before and after delayering

these activities we are able to conclude that the process took place rather rapidly and drastic intervention was not shunned. Attention was given, however, to sufficient support from the Supervisory Council in order to be able to change the 'power bases' within the concern.

Systematic investigation of costs

In order to be able to map out and subsequently reduce the indirect costs within the organization, a large-scale investigation of costs took place.

Changes in management positions

Over the last few years a total of 38 managing directors have left the group. Because the divisional staff were split up, the attrition rate of staff employees was also quite high. This is partly responsible for the large increase in added value per employee (see Figures 3.28 and 3.29).

Management after delayering

After delayering, the management of the subsidiaries was changed. Every subsidiary now reports to one of the members of the Board of Management. The managing directors of the subsidiaries have a large degree of freedom to act as they think appropriate, but must comply with a number of internal requirements. The Board of Management follows the performance of the subsidiaries and intervenes whenever a subsidiary does not come up to standard. Measurement of performance and rejection of subsidiaries which are not profitable enough are important factors in the overall management.

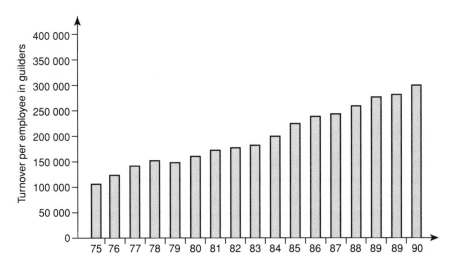

Figure 3.28   Net turnover per employee in guilders

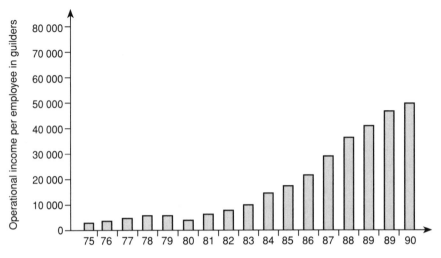

Figure 3.29   Net trading result per employee in guilders

Measuring performance

Elsevier has developed a system to measure the performance of the subsidiaries and groups. There are three concrete parameters:

- profit
- the PJV ratio (operational income/integral labour costs)
- the profit margin.

It is clear to anybody with responsibilities for a certain part that these are the parameters the Board of Management uses to measure performance. These parameters are furthermore stressed in the long-term plans and the operational budgets.

Rejection of insufficiently profitable activities

On completion of the merger, it appeared that a number of unprofitable activities remained. Provided they did not comply to the internal requirements for earning power, these activities were rejected. This was the fate of, amongst others, the newspaper *Het Vaderland*, and several printers. All general publishing houses were sold or closed.

Evaluation

We have evaluated the changes in the profit position since 1981. Figures 3.28 and 3.29 showed the relationship between the number of employees and the operational income (Figure 3.28) and the net turnover (Figure 3.29).

These relationships appear to be relevant to the degree of efficiency within the organization. The higher the amount of profit per employee, the more efficient the organization.

When looking at Figures 3.28 and 3.29, we can see that the turnover of Elsevier-NDU increased more or less continuously and that the net trading result per employee grew fastest between 1983 and 1985. These figures indicate that the profit per employee was highest in the period directly following the organizational changes. Because of the large number of variables involved, such as the large number of profitable acquisitions in the last ten years, it is difficult to establish what the exact contribution of the delayering process was to this increase.

Considering the large reduction in indirect costs while maintaining turnover, the direct increase in results since 1982, and the increased competitiveness of the group in those years, the financial and economic effect of the delayering operation can be classed as extremely positive.

The changes to the management are considered to be a clear improvement by Elsevier's top level. On the one hand, there is more freedom for managers and, on the other hand, the influence of the Board of Management reaches all the way to the front. Clear and concise standards exist and this is seen as very positive.

NBM-AMSTELLAND

This case study describes the delayering process which took place at NBM-Amstelland in 1991. The reason for the delayering was the merger between NV Verenigde NBM-bedrijven and Amstelland Concernbeheer BV. The delayering at NBM-Amstelland can be described as a delayering of the top which led to the abolition of the Management Council.

Brief description

NBM-Amstelland was formed in 1988 following the merger between NV Verenigde NBM-bedrijven and Amstelland Concernbeheer BV. Immediately after the merger, the Verenigde NBM-bedrijven's share in the Verenigde Tiemstra bedrijven was increased from 40 to 100 per cent.

Table 3.8 NBM-Amstelland's business statistics between 1988 and 1992

	1988	*1989*	*1990*	*1991*	*1992*
Group turnover[1]	1.522	1,609	1.813	1,857	1,942
Trading results[1]	35	46	33[2]	29[3]	34
No. of employees	5,327	5,177	4,989	5,033	4,763

[1] Amounts in millions of guilders
[2] Sold Amstelland Baksteengroep
[3] Sold Cleton Insulation BV

Following the merger, NBM-Amstelland was one of the three largest construction companies in the Netherlands. Its activities are split into the following market segments: utility, housing, dry hydraulics, project development and real estate, infrastructure, and environment.

The old top structure

After the merger, the NBM-Amstelland's structure consisted of the following groups:

- Road Construction
- Project Development
- Construction (amongst other things concrete for prefabricated houses)
- Commerce and Industry (manufacture of bricks, thermal insulation, etc.).

The groups comprised a number of independent companies. Above these groups of subsidiaries stood a large Management Council consisting of 11 members who were each directors of a number of companies within the groups.

The Management Council's main task was to co-ordinate the activities of the various subsidiaries. The Council was headed by the Board of Management, which consisted of four people of the former Boards of Management of NBM and Amstelland (see Figure 3.30).

This structure failed to function properly because the organization was still split into three 'blood types', a legacy of the original companies involved in the merger (NBM, Amstelland and Tiemstra). In the next section we will see that, apart from the structure not working properly, a number of other factors played a part in the decision to change.

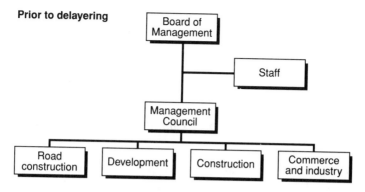

Figure 3.30   The structure of NBM-Amstelland prior to delayering

Reasons for delayering

Within NBM-Amstelland, a number of developments took place which directly or indirectly led to the Board of Management initiating a change process.

Ambiguous task definition

Following the merger, the Boards of Management of NBM and Amstelland were combined. In this period it became apparent that the necessary unity within the Board of Management was lacking. There was also confusion regarding tasks and authority and communication was problematic. The Board of Management did not adhere to the agreed task definition and communication with the operational level was not properly co-ordinated. The task of the Management Council was equally unclear. It seemed to have more of an honorary status.

An external investigation indicated a need for 'one captain on the ship'. The Supervisory Council saw itself faced with the difficult but important task of appointing a new Chairman for the Board of Management. The appointment of this new Chairman was the first step in the direction of the change process.

Differences in the business cultures of the partners in the merger

The most obvious difference between NBM and Amstelland was that Amstelland operated in a very decentralized way with financial direction from the Board of Management, while NBM was being managed from a more central level and more directly. The types of managers in each company also differed. NBM's directors were more building contractors and those at Amstelland were more general managers who were responsible for the results of their company within a clearly defined structure.

A certain amount of overlapping within the group, causing internal competition

After the merger, the organization comprised a number of construction companies which operated alongside each other in the same market segments. On a number of occasions, these sister companies were competing with each other for the same project. To avoid this type of overlap, the choice of an unambiguous decentralized management philosophy was followed in a reorganization by product group. Each company then knew which part of the market it was to serve. Because of this reorganization, the tasks and authorities of the Management Council also changed.

In short, the merger had led to a lack of unity within the group. This would eventually result in diminished returns and a reduced competitiveness and synergy, or, as someone put it, 'the organization started to decay'.

The new top structure

After a few changes in the top and a strategic reorientation the new Chairman of the Board of Management proposed a new organizational structure in May 1991. The main objective of this new structure was to concentrate on core business within a product-market group. The starting points for the new structure were an amalgamation of the various 'blood types' and the achievement of enough critical mass for each of the product-market groups.

The implementation of this new structure was a difficult phase. The subsidiaries were categorized into the new groups. On some occasions, a subsidiary was split up or merged with another, while others were rejected, closed down or rationalized. Within the groups, a number of regional agreements were made.

The new groups were:

- Infrastructure and Environment
- Project Development and Property
- Commercial and Industrial Construction

- Housing Construction
- Commerce and Supply.

These groups each have their own small management team of one or two people and a small administrative department. Above the group management teams is the Board of Management, which consists of three people.

The Board of Management, together with the group managment, constitutes the Corporate Management Council of NBM-Amstelland. The Board of Management consults with the group management during the meetings of the Corporate Management Council on policy-making and related matters. The new organizational structure is shown in Figure 3.31.

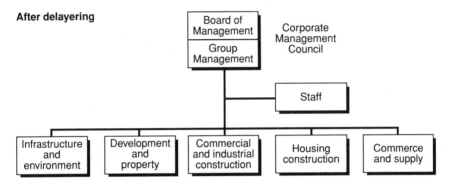

Figure 3.31 The structure of NBM-Amstelland after delayering

CHANGES TO THE ORGANIZATIONAL STRUCTURE

When looking at the present situation of NBM-Amstelland we can establish that the following changes have taken place:

- the organization changed from an ambiguous and not very obvious group model to a product-market orientated group model
- the Management Council, which had no obvious organizational task, has disappeared
- each group has its own financial and legal structure within which the financially and legally independent subsidiaries operate
- the Board of Management and the chairmen of each group's management consult with each other in the Corporate Management Council on matters such as, policy, continuation and developments in the market.

- the management of each group lies with a management team consisting of members from each subsidiary in the group under the leadership of a chairman who has final responsibility for all the goings on in that group
- the corporate staff has been reduced in size.

The main consequences of delayering have thus been the disappearance of the Management Council, the changes to the role of the Board of

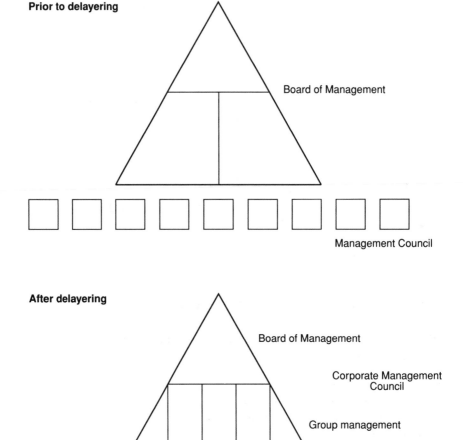

Figure 3.32   Composition and division of tasks of NBM-Amstelland before and after delayering

Management and the Corporate Management Council and the composition of the Corporate Management Council. Because the Board of Management and the group management have been partially merged into the Corporate Management Council the organization of NBM-Amstelland has become flatter (see Figure 3.32)

Supporting measures

In order to realize the changes in structure and render them effective, a number of measures have been taken. The most remarkable ones are listed below.

Strategic leadership

The appointment of a new Chairman of the Board of Management has been a very important step in the delayering process at NBM-Amstelland.

The corporate plan which was drawn up by this new Chairman gave direction to the delayering process. The Chairman also discussed this plan with the new key figures in the organization and adapted it where necessary.

Altering the company culture

The two merged companies complemented each other as far as products were concerned; their cultures, however, varied enormously. The way in which managers were assessed as well as the standards and values were very different from each other. The culture of planning, evaluation and assessment has received a great deal of attention and a reward system was introduced.

Selection of key figures

Another important step in the change process was the selection of group managing directors for the Corporate Council. Even before the change in the company culture, this selection would have been important. The chairmen of the group management teams and the members of the Central Employee Participation Council were seen by the Board of Management as important figures in channelling the change process in the right direction within the groups. The Central Employee Participation Council was extended from 13 to 26 members to increase the basis for the changes.

Adjustment of structure

The new structure has been formally, financially and legally established at NBM-Amstelland. Each subsidiary has had to conform to this structure. Creating clarity regarding the financial and legal responsibility and the hierarchical relationship was a response to the existing uncertainty.

The delayering process

In the previous sections an indication was given of how the structure had changed and which measures were taken to realize the delayering. Below we will briefly describe how this process transpired.

The first step in the delayering process was undoubtedly the appointment of a new Chairman of the Board of Management in May 1991. This Chairman immediately introduced a plan for the change process. It was imperative to resolve the ambiguity surrounding tasks, responsibilities and authority in the entire organization. From the existing management, a number of suitable people were chosen on the basis of their ability to give the change process shape. At the same time, the subsidiaries were reorganized. The groups into which the subsidiaries were organized, as well as the subsidiaries themselves, were given their own financial and legal structures.

The approach was top down. The change process continues. Some groups and subsidiaries are still trying to 'get the ship on course'.

Evaluation of the delayering

The delayering at NBM-Amstelland has been a laborious process and it has not yet been completed. The process has seen a few critical moments. One of those moments was the period prior to the appointment of the new Chairman of the Board of Management. During that period the 'top figures' experienced some uncertainty and ambiguity regarding the future of the organization and its staffing. After the Chairman had been appointed and new key figures had been selected, the consequences of the new policy caused some resistance. The reorganization of the subsidiaries, which involved closures, rationalizations, divisions and mergers, was very traumatic.

The process does, however, appear to be showing some results. At the moment, there is more clarity within the group regarding the operational management. Groups have been formed around a core business, the introduction of the new house style has ensured a clearer profiling and all this has led to more unity within the concern. Responsibilities have been fixed in the structure and there are clear performance requirements on which the groups are assessed.

Several issues still have a high priority. First, the *collective achievements* in the Corporate Management Council as a result of the change process will be spread throughout the subsidiaries. The more clarity is created regarding objectives, structures, tasks and responsibilities, the better group directors are able to lead their group by delegation. This should provide scope and time which can be dedicated to corporate interests.

Second, the Board of Management will look at its own tasks and added value within this new, more independent, company. This means that they have to put into action the concept of synergy.

The forms of synergy that can be distinguished are:

- exchange of market information between groups
- exchange of technology and operational expertise (management development, quality)
- co-operation between groups on points were their own maximum performance in the commercial field and in the area of product-market combinations can be surpassed.

The prerequisite for making these forms of synergy work is that every group management team has 'its own ship on course'. This is not yet the case within every group.

The final result of the change process will only become apparent in a few years' time. However, the present results do give reason to be hopeful.

ASEA BROWN BOVERI

In this case, we describe the process of delayering at ABB. The reason for delayering was the cross-border merger in August 1987 between two engineering groups: Asea (Swedish) and Brown Boveri (Swiss). The process of delayering took place at the top.

Brief description of the situation before the merger

Asea, founded in 1891, was, until 1980, just a sleepy electrical engineering firm with 50 per cent of its business in Sweden and only a marginal presence in the EC markets. The appointment, in 1980, of Mr Percy Barnevik as CEO was the beginning of some interesting changes.

Barnevik wanted to enlarge the basis of Asea. He launched a series of bold acquisitions to expand Asea's businesses, first in Scandinavia and then in North America and Asia, and he cut the headquarters' staff to a reasonable size (2,000). By the end of 1987, Mr Barnevik had achieved a four-fold (to $9 billion) increase in Asea's sales; a ten-fold increase in earnings; and boosted its market capitalization 20 times. Under his leadership, Asea became one of the largest robot producers, (number two in the world). But, despite reorganization, concentration and acquisitions, Asea was still very dependent on the Scandinavian market, which accounted for more than half of its sales. Mr Barnevik, therefore, made a merger proposal to BBC Brown Boveri, a Swiss competitor.

BBC Brown Boveri, founded in 1883, was a well-respected company with large customer bases in Germany and the US. It employed 94,000 people and had 4,000 headquarters' staff in Baden. BBC possessed great expertise in top-of-the-range technology and had a strong market position in West Germany and Switzerland. It produced high-quality goods, but generally launched them too late. The profit margin had become dangerously low because of overstaffing and internal competition. Before the merger, Brown Boveri had two 'dividend free' years.

Overstaffing

BBC employed a large number of old-style managers. Due to the commitment to State power activities, the managers took too few risks and were afraid to cut jobs.

Internal competition

BBC was a federation of empires, each with its own policy. Because of its size (35,000 employees), the German operation was the most powerful. There were even rivalries with the Swiss parent. The major R&D spending at BBC was not always tied to commercial needs, but was de-coupled instead.

Reasons for the merger

The merger is the result of Mr Barnevik's vision. In his opinion, the European industry of heavy electrical engineering was in a 'no win' situation: Europe only has room for three or four major electrical groups and he wanted Asea to be one of them.

Table 3.9 Facts and figures of BBC and ASEA in 1986

	BBC	*ASEA*
Orders received*	11 billion	11.2 billion
Turnover*	13 billion	11 billion
Profits*	213 million	603 million
R&D*	1,095 million	365 million
Investments	560 million	1 billion
Employees	94,000	71,000

* In Swiss francs

Asea had to become one of the leading electro-technical companies in the world. To achieve this goal, Asea pursued the North European strategy. Asea spread their production and development activities over the whole of Scandinavia. By merging with BBC, the North-European strategy could be realized at once because BBC had companies in Norway and Denmark. Asea's main reason for the merger was expansion. For BBC, the merger meant more market orientation, élan and clarity.

The merger of Asea with BBC meant that a reorganization of the European electronical business was necessary because:

- it was overcrowded with 20 large and medium-sized national companies
- there was an overcapacity of up to 50 per cent.

The demand for power generation, power distribution and transportation equipment in Europe only grows 0.66 per cent a year and the market will not pick up before the mid 1990s. In the meantime, the electro-technical business has to cope with overcapacity, on a world-wide scale of 30 to 40 per cent. ABB's main competitors' answer to this problem was to diversify into consumer electronics, defence equipment, even medical products to reduce their dependence on electrical engineering in general and the power industry in particular. However, ABB stuck to their core business: power. Furthermore:

- the cost structure is much too high
- half of the industry leads a marginal existence or is loss-making.

The catalyst to merger between Asea and BBC was 'the borderless Europe of 1993'. The European electro-technical companies are publicly owned or heavily subsidized. They were largely operating in markets which were closed to foreigners. As a result there was no cross-border traffic within the EC and certainly not to the US and Japan. The electro-technical business in Europe could not compete with the American or Japanese. Mr Barnevik wanted to create a group which was founded in Europe, but with joint ventures or preferably 100 per cent-owned acquisitions links with the US and Japan.

By means of mergers and joint ventures, Mr Barnevik works towards three goals:

- strengthening the company's position in Europe
- penetration of the American market
- becoming active in Asia from the inside, not as an outsider.

Short description of ABB

ABB – Asea Brown Boveri Ltd. – is owned in equal parts by Asea AB, Stockholm, Sweden, and BBC Brown Boveri Ltd., Baden, Switzerland. Asea Brown Boveri Ltd., Zurich, is the holding company of the Asea Brown Boveri Group with approximately 1,300 companies around the world. Power generation, distribution and use are the core businesses of ABB.

ABB is the largest supplier to the world's electricity industry. In 1992, the largest individual contract since ABB's formation was received from Abu Dhabi for an $800 million combined steam power station and desalination plant.

Table 3.10 Revenue per region

	1992	1991
Europe/EC*	11,147	10,302
Europe/EFTA*	6,320	7,038
North America-NAFTA*	4,931	4,350
Asia/Australia*	4,927	4,350
South America/Africa/E. Europe*	2,290	1,928
Total*	29,615	28,883

* US$ in millions

Niche opportunities in ABB's other businesses are being opened by its excellent R&D effort. It now even competes with Japan in the manufacture of industrial robots. In locomotives, ABB is already the main 'domestic' supplier to the Swiss, Scandinavian and West German railways. ABB has produced a tilting high-speed train that operates on existing tracks, thus cutting costs. ABB is a leader in high-voltage DC transmission, which reduces the costs of transmitting power over long distances. ABB, furthermore, is a leader in pollution control equipment. More than half of ABB's sales are in Europe, about a fifth in North America, and the remainder in Asia, South America and Africa.

Since October 1993, ABB has been divided into four product segments (power plants, power transmission and building systems, transportation) and three geographical regions (Europe, the Americas, and Asia and the Pacific).

ABB pursues the following strategy.

- *Think global, act local* They balance the contradictions of staying both local *and* global. The idea for each national subsidiary of ABB is to act as a domestic company. Manufacturing is specialized between countries to gain economies of scale, but assembly and engineering is often done locally. ABB has local customer bases that reap the advantages of global economies of scale, world-wide co-ordination and the ability to tap into the technological and R&D support systems represented by the many companies that feed ABB's main businesses.
- *Big and small*
- *Radically decentralized with centralized reporting and control*
- *Technological leadership* R&D is held at a constant level, about 8 per cent of revenues. Competitors spend around 5 per cent. Mr Barnevik says, 'you have to be in command of your destiny in your core technologies'. For ABB, one core technology is power semiconductors (electronic switching devices for high-voltage transmission). ABB is 'customer pulled' rather than 'technology pushed'.

Delayering at ABB

The organizational structure before delayering

Six or seven years before the merger, Asea had a matrix structure. BBC had a geographical structure that had to be converted into a product divisional structure. BBC did not possess an effective matrix organization. In many

Table 3.11 Key figures of ABB

	1988	1989	1990	1991	1992
Orders received*	17,822	21,640	29,281	29,621	31,634
Revenues*	17,832	20,560	26,688	28,883	29,615
Operating earnings*†	854	1,257	1,790	1,908	1,810
Earnings after financial items*	560	922	1,130	1,153	1,110
Net income*	386	589	590	609	505
Employees*	169,459	189,493	215,154	214,393	213,407

* US$ in millions (ABB uses a single currency for all its consolidated global financial reporting – the US dollar)
† After depreciation

Table 3.12 Data per business segment (US$ in millions)

Business segment	Orders received		Revenues		Operating earnings after depreciation	
	1992	1991	1992	1991	1992	1992
Power plants	8,322	7,997	6,947	6,820	444	366
Power transmission	5,818	5,528	5,606	5,514	520	513
Power distribution	3,518	3,274	3,345	3,196	175	174
Industry	4,935	4,230	4,430	4,486	184	271
Transportation	2,896	2,093	2,662	1,946	−40	21
Financial services	805	868	805	868	228	148
Various activities	9,945	9,641	10,027	9,740	368	489

countries each subsidiary had its own management structure, undertook its own marketing, research and production, thus duplicating costs and dissipating strategy.

Motives for delayering

After the merger an organization would arise with too steep a top structure. Mr Barnevik foresaw several bottlenecks and cut drastically the number of headquarters staff. The external motives for delayering were similar to the motives for the merger and are listed below.

External developments

- increasing competition
- excess capacity in the electrical equipment industry in Europe
- globalization of markets.

Internal developments

- huge headquarters staff, duplication of functions at headquarters
- improving market orientation, enhancing customer service
- aiming to achieve technological leadership
- flexibility
- drastically reducing production time
- improving quality
- improving communication
- internal competition.

The process of delayering

The process of delayering started right after the merger. Mr Barnevik chose a fast integral scenario of change. He was the initiator and leader of this process and was interested in keeping the period of uncertainty as short as possible. All major changes were undertaken in the first year of the merger.

After the merger, Mr Barnevik chose a two step strategy: first, restructuring, then growth.

1 *Restructuring/integration (1987)* ABB's headquarters are based in Zurich. Of the 2,500 subsidiaries, 100 were closed after the merger and 200 were integrated. Activities were swapped from one business area to another. R&D was concentrated in three main centres (Vasteras, Heidelberg and Baden) and six smaller ones. Their cohesion is essential to ABB's aim to become the low-cost producer in all of its businesses.

2 *Delayering of the top (1987)* Headquarters staff was cut drastically, from 4,000 to 200 in Baden, from 900 to 88 in the US, from 1,600 to 100 in Germany (Mannheim) and from 880 to 25 in Finland (Stromberg). Their US acquisition, Combustion Engineering, based in Stamford, was advised to reduce its staff from 600 to 100. Asea had a headquarters staff of 2,000

people in Västeras (Sweden) and BBC 4,000 people in Baden before the merger. The combined company now has a headquarters staff of 150 in Zurich.

Table 3.13 Mr Barnevik's corporate overhead guideline

Year 1: 90% reduction in headquarter	
● 30%	lay-off and/or attrition
● 30%	to profit centers
● 30%	to service centers operating/competing at market prices
● 10%	remaining corporate staff
−/−30%	
Year 3–4: further attack . . .	
● service centers down to 15% (reduced by half)	
● profit centers down to 20% (cut by a third)	
● corporate center down to 5% (reduced by half)	
−/−30%	

Result: After two rounds of cuts 60% of the staff is eliminated and only 5% will remain in the corporate center.

3 *The profit centres operation* This operation became an independent power within BBC; the establishment of many profit centres. The profit centres have a great deal of autonomy in purchasing and will be close to their markets and customers (which means short decision lines).

4 *Acquisition (1988–1991)* After the merger, the group went on an acquisition spree. Mr Barnevik insists that the head count involved in any headquarters activity can be cut by 90 per cent in the first year, following the above-mentioned corporate overhead guideline. The period of huge acquisitions is now over for ABB. Since 1992, there has been a period of consolidation, selective growth and sharp costs reductions.

5 *Customer Focus Programme* This programme is intended to improve quality, shorten production and delivery times and increase productivity. In Sweden it takes the form of a T50 (time minus 50 per cent) campaign which aims to halve throughput time in all group operations, whether manufacturing or administrative, by 1993. In 1992 ABB had more than 800 Customer Focus Programmes around the world.

Many ABB companies are still structured in the traditional way, with functional departments – sales, design, production, distribution. The

Table 3.14 ABB's acquisitions and divestments

Year	Acquisitions		Divestments	
	Number	Amount in US$m	Number	Amount in US$m
1988	16	544	5	171
1989	39	3,090	10	64
1990	37	677	17	1,078
1991	34	612	23	607
1992	126	4,923	55	1,920

structural objective of T50 is to completely flip the primary axis of doing business, getting almost everyone – representing all functions – out of the specialist departments and into 'horizontal' product divisions consisting of 30 to 100 people. The final step is to further decompose those 30- to 100-person product divisions into ten-person High-performance Teams.

New organizational structure

ABB's favoured description, rather than 'multinational', is 'multidomestic', which more aptly defines its highly decentralized national operations.

ABB is a matrix structure with countries and industries as the two dimensions. Individual profit centres, plants and companies within a 'country structure' constitute one dimension of the matrix, business areas (BAs) make up the other.

The domestic part of ABB's 'multidomestic' character is provided by the dimension 'countries' of the matrix (ABB Germany, ABB France and so on) with their own presidents and Boards, operating as would any other local corporation – with supervisory Boards in Germany, for example.

The two parts of the matrix intersect at the level of the group's 1,300 companies, whose heads both report to their national Company President and their BA Leader, wherever they may be based.

At the top of ABB is an eight-member Executive Committee, which is headed by Mr Barnevik. Some committee members are responsible for each of the five business segments into which 50 BAs are consolidated. Others have regional or functional responsibilities, and some have a combination of

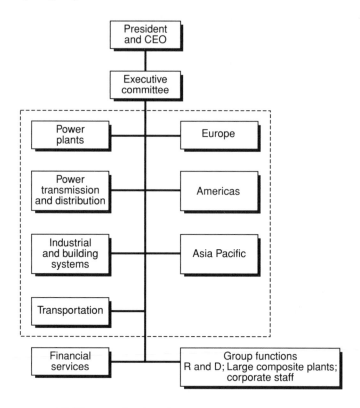

Figure 3.33   ABB's organizational structure

both. The BAs and business segments are responsible for the global production activities. The BA leader does not double as a company president, but
performs the BA task full-time and is supported by a small team. BA teams
range in size from one (or less, a part-time company president) to ten or 15.
The BA manager is responsible for optimizing the business on a global basis.
It is their job to devise and champion a global strategy, to hold the factories
in their business area to cost and quality standards, to allocate their export
markets and to develop truly international management talent by rotating
people across borders, create mixed-nationality teams to solve problems
and build a culture of multinational trust.

   Along the other dimension in the matrix there are the countries, each with
a country manager who reports to a member of the Executive Committee.
Within the countries, there is a total of some 1,300 independently incorporated companies. These companies are divided into some 5,000 profit

centres. These profit centres are responsible for the sales. At the 'bottom', the profit centres are beginning to reorganize into ten-person, multi-functional High-performance Teams. The centres are run collectively by 5,000 profit-responsible individuals in teams of three or four.

ABB has three layers of management: the Executive Committee, below this level come 250 senior executives, including 100 country managers and most of the BA chiefs, then the 5,000 profit centre managers with their management teams.

Supporting measures

Strategic leadership

Mr Barnevik is the motivator of the reorganization and delayering that takes/took place at ABB. He is the leader of the Executive Committee with the strategic vision. The BA managers are crucial people. They craft strategy, evaluate performance around the world and work with teams made up of different nationalities.

Supporting performance information system

A management information system called Abacus provides centralized reporting on the group's 5,000 profit centres and 1,200 companies each month. Abacus compares the collected data with budgets and forecasts, converts them into dollars to enable cross-border analysis, and consolidates or breaks them down by segment, country and local company.

An ambitious new quality goal and measurement system (called 10-UP-s) has been set up for the company's quality improvement process. The plan calls for 'step-function' improvements of 50 per cent or better in ten key areas each year in all businesses.

Common parameters are set for all the companies operating within each business area; irrespective of where it is based, a company's monthly performance is measured in a 'league table' against that of all other companies in its BA. Each BA has its own management board, composed of the heads of leading national companies, which meets up to six times a year.

Key managers in the organization

Some committee members are responsible for each of the five business segments into which 50 BAs are consolidated. Others have regional or functional responsibilities, and some have a combination of both. The BA leader does not double as a company president

Meetings of the Executive Committee are held every three weeks in a different country. Each BA has its own management board, composed of heads of leading national companies, which meets up to six times a year. Less often, perhaps once or twice a year, functional co-ordination teams meet to exchange ideas and information on such matters as production, quality and marketing.

Entrepreneurship

ABB consists of 5,000 autonomous operating units (profit centres).

Contracting of suppliers

ABB is developing a family of suppliers for each of its businesses. Mr Barnevik does not care where they are. His supplier network helps him to cut product cycle times, which he believes will help unlock future profits. The global search for suppliers sometimes leads ABB into countries that less internationally minded companies shun. ABB was one of the first into Poland after capitalism took root, buying two State-owned factories that manufacture turbines and other power-generating equipment.

Selection of global managers

ABB needs 500 global managers from among 15,000 managers to make ABB work. The successful manager, according to Mr Barnevik, needs patience, good language ability, stamina, work experience in at least two or three countries and, most importantly, humility. Stamina may be more useful for those who work for the company.

Powerful factors that encourage the ABB melting pot are:

- Mr Barnevik's insistence that all senior managers, particularly those involved in international dealings, use English in any written and spoken communication
- according to Mr Barnevik, global managers are made, not born – the way to create global managers is job rotation around the world, people are encouraged to work in mixed-nationality teams and forced to create personal alliances across borders.

Change of culture

ABB has set out its values in a 40-page booklet. This includes ethics, individual responsibility and initiative and openness to foreign cultures.

ABB's Customer Focus Programme is permanently changing the value system of ABB and orientating every employee to the customer. A Customer Focus Information Desk has been founded that is concerned with the collecting and (internal) publishing of all achieved successes of ABB, which focus on production improvements and shorter production times.

Evaluation and future perspectives

ABB has become a truly global group, with local roots in more than 100 countries.

ABB has not only become the single largest supplier to the world's electricity industry, it is also a leading world supplier of robots, process automation systems, locomotives and air pollution equipment.

The multidomestic company ABB has to deal with some major problems.

- A problem in any huge organization is communication. It is hard to communicate clearly and quickly to tens of thousands of people around the world. To cope with this problem, people are overinformed, because European managers have a strong tendency to be selective about sharing information.
- The 'two bosses' problem (BA manager and country manager). To be sure, there is a formal mechanism for conflict resolution: each BA manager reports to one of the 13 members of the Executive Committee and so does each country manager (ordinarily they report to different country managers).
- ABB has difficulties in finding/creating global managers; it is a crucial bottleneck.

1992 was the fifth year following the formation of the ABB group. In these five years, order intake grew by 78 per cent. In 1992, ABB was affected by an international environment marked by both stagnation and increasingly fierce competition.

For its future ABB is firmly tied to the electrics business: the generation, distribution and usage of electricity. The future of ABB is based on the expectation of Mr Barnevik that electricity demand will grow and major investments will be made in Asia, where the strongest growth is expected. However, if the expected growth does not materialize, the brutal price-cutting he has made possible could come back to haunt him. A drastic drop in earnings from power would leave ABB with few other life lines. On the other hand, Barnevik has said ABB's aim is to become the low-cost supplier who can survive profitably even with low growth.

1994 will be the fourth year of recession in Western Europe. The goals of ABB, however, remain to achieve a 10 per cent average operating earnings margin and a 25 per cent return on capital within a few years.

4

A MANAGER'S INSTRUMENTS FOR DELAYERING

We have seen a number of examples of companies that have decided to reduce the distance between top and shop floor. The results of this peek behind the scenes of nine organizations are analysed in this and following chapters.

An important difference was that, in particular, the management layers of the top were arranged differently in a number of organizations, such as GE, Akzo, Elsevier and NBM-Amstelland. At DAC, Hoogovens, AEGON and Avéro Verzekeringen we have seen that the operational processes were organized differently. DAC, for instance, was working on a TQMS programme in combination with defunctionalization towards product and process orientation. This led to a gigantic restructuring which resulted in a delayering of the structure, and to a far-reaching change in culture.

At Avéro Verzekeringen the restructuring and change in culture was related to a reorganization of the top. At Hoogovens a decision was taken within production management to rearrange the structure. At both organizations the structure was tilted and underwent a reorientation: from an organization arranged around functions they changed to an organization arranged around products or markets.

In these cases, we saw that there was a difference between delayering of the top and delayering of the middle management. The actions taken by Akzo and GE, where management layers in the top have been merged, differ from the actions taken by, for instance, AEGON and DAC. These differences are outlined in Figure 4.1 (90).

Not only are there differences in the structuring measures. The supporting measures contributing to the new structure being able to actually function also differ between delayering of the top and delayering of middle management. We will therefore discuss the instruments for delayering that managers have at their disposition in two separate sections. In each section we will look at the various roles the concern, including the division, or the middle management can take. In practice, it has appeared that if the group and the division opt for a certain role, this influences the delayering options. Delayering of the middle management requires a different way of organizing which actually affects the roles of this middle management.

We conclude this chapter with observations which may lead managers to consider, or start with, delayering.

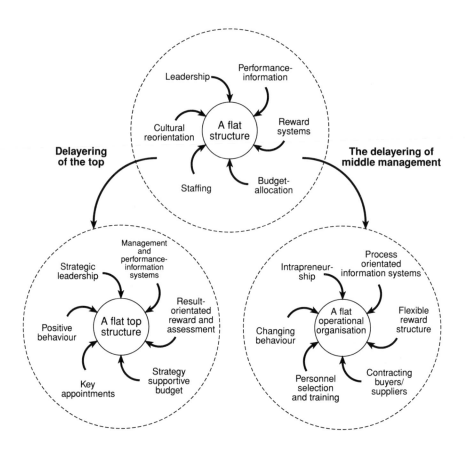

Figure 4.1   Delayering themes

DELAYERING OF THE TOP

Delayering of the top is often not an easy topic of discussion. As every layer attracts power and staff, many managers and employees will dig in and so resist any changes in general and delayering in particular. Jack Welch indicates that structure is a good starting point for change: 'First we took out management layers. Layers hide weaknesses. Layers mask mediocrity'. In practice, the initiative to delayer the concern's top is, therefore, taken at the highest level: by the Chairman of the Board of Management. Only if he or she is sufficiently persistent, has the operation a chance of succeeding. The unconditional support of the Board of Directors or Supervisory Council is also considered to be absolutely imperative. In this section we discuss the overall, concern, management and staff functions, the options for structuring the top and the measures being taken to enhance the effects of changes to the top structure.

Roles of the concern

Delayering of the top plays a particularly important role in organizations servicing several product-market combinations. This is particularly the case for concerns consisting of several divisions with strategic business units and groups of business units or subsidiaries underneath them.

All organizations that have reduced the number of management layers in the top also show a change in the role of the concern. The operational co-ordinating role of the concern becomes less all-encompassing. Co-ordination moves from the divisional level to the Board of Management, whereby a number of Board members carry responsibility for the business units. On the one hand, we thus see a centralization of responsibility because someone from the Board of Management is accountable. On the other hand, we see that responsibilities are delegated to the business units.

According to Daems and Douma, the concern can add value to the business units in terms of five roles: as investor, as restructurer, as adviser, as co-ordinator or as defender (15).

As investor

The role of capital provider can be found predominantly in conglomerates and investment companies. The added value lies in the fact that a large concern is often able to attract capital with more favourable conditions than smaller units can.

In addition, the concern, in its role of capital provider, is able to allocate funds to units with the best potential for profit. After all, the concern's top often receives more or better information than an external provider of capital. The concern acts, in fact, as a shareholder and, in this capacity, requires proper insight into the performance of the subsidiaries. When this is the concern's main role, it is possible to work with a small holding group in relation to the number of business units.

As restructurer

Having experience in assessing the possibilities of companies in trouble is an opportunity for the concern to add value. In its purest form, a concern buys companies, restructures these and then sells them off again. In a number of cases this is the concern's role with regard to business units that are not sufficiently profitable. It is also possible for the concern to take the initiative during a reorganization or strengthening of certain units.

A number of entrepreneurs have a great deal of experience in restructuring organizations or organizational units in trouble. It also occurs that a concern employs managers who are sent out as 'troubleshooters' to companies experiencing difficulties. From the point of view of delayering, the role of restructurer is only a temporary one. Once the restructuring is rounded off, the business unit is either sold or will go its own way under its own steam within the concern.

As adviser

Organizations specializing in a certain area – such as financial services or the production and marketing of chemical products – often contain a vast amount of expertise in highly specialist areas. These concerns in particular can add value by acting as advisers. Even certain support functions, such as information technology and management development, can combine their specialist knowledge, on the basis of which, advice can be offered to the business units.

In general, it can be said that the stronger the relationship between the business units, the more added value the concern can provide by acting as adviser. As a result of this role of the concern, staff departments tend to grow. A good division of tasks, responsibilities and authority is then required. Should this role decrease in importance, it often appears that an additional layer which has to approve the business units' actions has been introduced. The role of adviser can be assumed either at a central level by the concern or at a decentralized level by the division (acting as a strategic business unit).

As co-ordinator

When the concern or the divisions assume the role of co-ordinator, they have a number of operational responsibilities. Co-ordination is possible in a number of areas such as logistics, production, product development, marketing, use of brand names and service. The concern can also co-ordinate supporting activities such as information technology, financial management or human resources management. If the concern co-ordinates activities, it can add value by giving more units access to expensive or unique facilities. The total costs are so reduced. However, if the concern gets a bigger say in the management of the business units, extra management layers tend to be created.

As defender

A business unit which operates only in one area of business or one country becomes relatively vulnerable to actions by competitors. Suppose that a foreign competitor manages to penetrate the domestic market of a business unit by starting a price war. It will, in this situation, be easier for the concern to make a counter move. This move may consist of starting a price war in the domestic market of the competitor. In this way the concern can defend the interests of the business unit. From the point of view of delayering, this role is less relevant.

In Box 4.1 we have outlined the above roles and the effect they can be expected to have on the steepness of the top structure.

In addition to the relation of the role of the concern to the number of layers in the top, the costs of the concern including the division are also important with regard to the opportunity to add value.

Daems and Douma indicate that there are four factors which determine the concern's advantage: the concern's costs, the concern's structure, consistency of the portfolio and added value of the concern. With regard to delayering, it is the latter which is particularly important. The concern, including the divisions, can add value in a number of roles. These different roles entail different costs. The costs of the concern and divisions can be split into three components. First, there are the costs of the headquarters – personnel costs, accommodation (this is exclusive of the costs which the business units would have had anyway). Second, there are the costs made by

Box 4.1   Roles of the concern and divisions

Role	Added value	Optimum structure
Investor	Concern is able to attract capital with more favourable conditions	Flat
Restructurer	Concern has specialist knowledge in restructuring or can provide optimum management capacity	Flat with temporary intervention by the concern
Adviser	Concern can offer specialist knowledge which can be used by the business units	Flat/tall (risk of extra layers)
Co-ordinator	Concern or divisions have the authority and size to carry out or co-ordinate collective tasks	Tall
Defender	Defending the interests of the business units	Flat with incidental support from the concern

the business units by providing information to the concern. The third type of costs do not appear on the balance sheet. They are the profit opportunities which are missed because the concern did not allow the development of certain activities. These costs are also referred to as *opportunity costs*.

There is no quick and ready answer to the question 'What is the best role for the concern?' After all, this differs from one situation to another. It is, however, essential that costs are made visible as far as possible. The costs of the concern hereby have to be in agreement with the added value of the concern.

A large-scale study by The Conference Board Europe also looked into the role of the concern (92).

Box 4.2 lists to what extent members of The Conference Board Europe thought that the concern had 'reserved powers' in certain areas.

This study clearly shows that the role of the concern changes. A small concern has a more measurable added value, a shift in influence towards the operational units, a greater streamlining of resources, people and information between units in a network, empowerment, and less direct intervention.

In addition to roles and content influencing potential, the concern can also

Box 4.2   Areas where the concern has reserved powers

Function	Mentions (maximum 20)
Strategy	18
Finance	12
Senior human resource policies	10
Corporate identity	9
Tax	8
Law	8
Management development	7
Communications	6
Investments	6
Acquisitions	5
Ethics	4
Community relations	4
Investor relations	4
Auditing	4
Alliances	3
Budgeting	3
Health, safety and environment	3
Organization	3
Quality	2
IT strategy	2

take different positions with regard to managerial control and vision concerning the degree of business integration (92). Figure 4.2 reflects the management style relating to this position.

In practice, we see that it is never really a choice, once and for all, of one position. The complex choice of structure involves taking into account the role of the concern, the concern's focus points and its views on management style. All these factors together lead to a choice of structure.

Possibilities for structuring the top

There is no 'one, best way' to structure the top of an organization. The choice of roles of the concern does determine, to a large extent, the possibility of delayering. Changing the top structure always leads to 'new disadvantages'. There will always be internal contradictions which have to be solved. For instance, at ABB: 'We want to be global and local, big and small, radically decentralized with centralized reporting and control. If we resolve

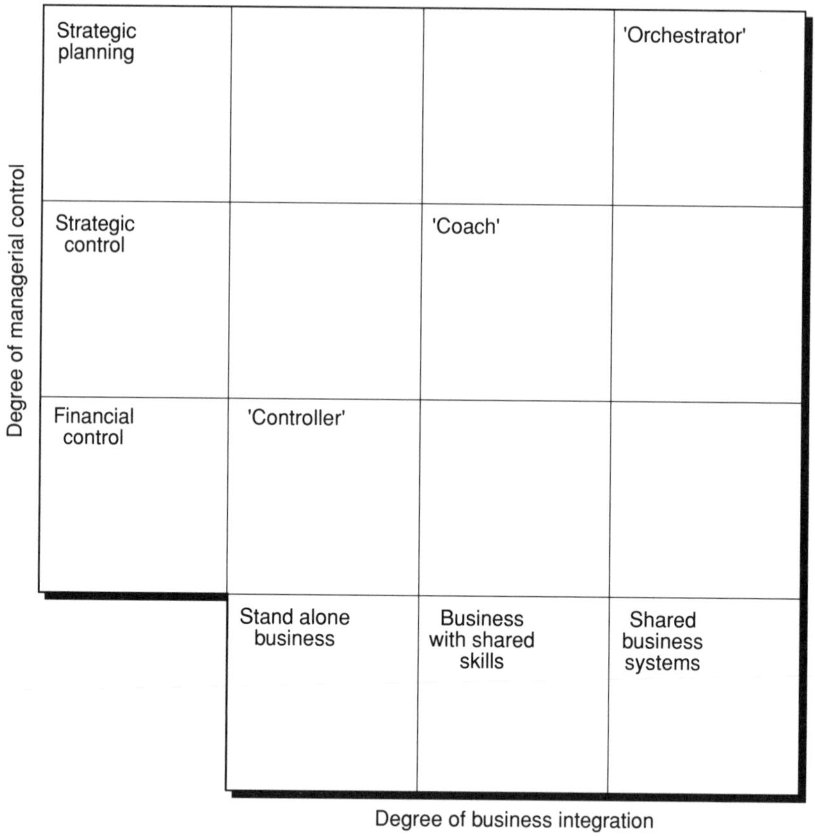

Figure 4.2   *Management styles of the centre (adapted from The Conference Board Europe, The Role of the Centre)*

those contradictions, we create a real organizational advantage'. We will, therefore, discuss the strategic advantages and disadvantages of a top structured on a *functional* basis, on a *divisional* basis, and on the basis of *business units*. We will indicate for each situation the possibilities for delayering.

The top structure in functional organizations

Figure 4.3 gives an example of a functional top structure for a production company and an insurance company. One of the people we interviewed commented with regard to this top structure: 'In our organization it was not clear who was responsible for what. A common problem always became someone else's problem. This, combined with the large amount of deliberation at management level, was, for us, one of the reasons to change'.

Example of manufacturing company

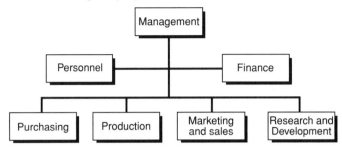

Example of insurance company

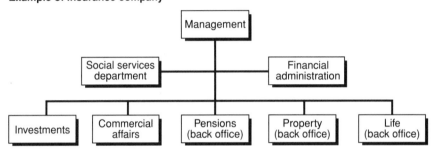

Figure 4.3   Top structures for functional organizations

A functional structure works best when the aim is to service a single product-market combination as efficiently as possible. The accent lies on concentration and use of the available resources. Within the present market situations in which flexibility in the product supply, long-term thinking, the speed at which decisions are made, and innovative capacity are increasingly important, it happens less and less that an organization is only concerned with *one* product-market combination. In a number of cases, a total reorientation of the functional structure into a product- or market-orientated divisional or business unit structure takes place.

In the case of a functional top structure we are not actually dealing with a concern. The role of the top consists, to a large extent, of co-ordination. This requires a substantial amount of time and attention. The high costs involved in this have to be earned back through increased efficiency. In Box 4.3 the advantages and disadvantages of the functional top structure are listed.

The possibilities for delayering the top of a functional organization are limited. One of the characteristics of this structure is, after all, the fact that

Box 4.3   Advantages and disadvantages of a functional top structure

Advantages	Disadvantages
• Suitable for one product-market combination	• Problems caused by functional co-ordination
• Central control	• Problems of market orientation
• Key activities in departments	• Rivalry between the various functions
• Functional expertise and specialization	• Over-specialization
• Efficiency created by routine jobs	• Limited development of integral management capacity
• High degree of capacity utilization	• Only top has responsibility for profits
• Steep learning curve	• Functional empires ('silos')
	• Limited entrepreneurship and innovation

the top plays an important role in the co-ordination. Within functional organizations it is possible, however, to reduce the number of management layers in middle management. This forms the theme of the section on delayering of the middle management.

Changing a functional structure into a product- or market-orientated structure provides ample scope for delayering because the co-ordination point moves downward in the organization.

Divisional or SBU structure

Figure 4.4 gives a schematic representation of a divisional structure – or a Strategic Business Unit (SBU) structure. This structure comprises an additional management layer in between top and business units. Below this divisional layer the various business units are grouped on the basis of related activities.

At one of the organizations where delayering consisted of cutting out the divisional layer, the Chairman commented: 'An organization structured around divisions is as a car which does have a steering wheel, but where

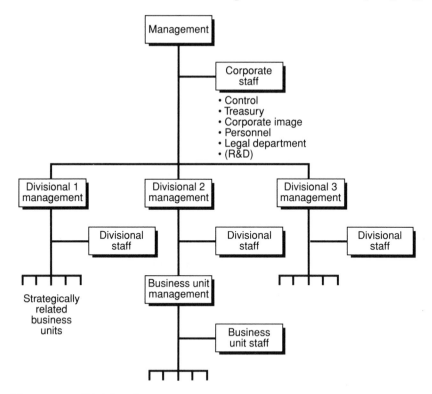

Figure 4.4   Divisional structure

turning this steering wheel only has a limited effect on the directions of the wheels. What bothered me in particular was those staff at various levels which effectively blocked decision making'.

Potential advantages of the divisional layer are related to synergy in the case of related activities. The divisions then fulfil the role of either adviser or co-ordinator. This does mean, however, that some very high costs are attached to the divisional layer. The division has to earn back these costs by adding value.

The other side of the picture is that a division often has the tendency to gather power by creating its own staff, which often develops quickly. This results in an increase in the distance between top and shop floor. The advantages of synergy are thus destroyed by higher costs at divisional level. One of the managers indicated that divisions acted too much as 'control bureaucracy'; the added value of this excessive control was called into doubt.

The added value of the divisional layer can decrease, partly because information technology allows the business units to be monitored directly from the top, or because the strategic management capacity of the business units themselves increases.

In Box 4.4 the advantages and disadvantages of a divisional structure are displayed.

Box 4.4   Advantages and disadvantages of a divisional structure

Advantages	Disadvantages
• Enhanced synergy and co-ordination for the business units • Coherence between related activities • Allocation of capacity on basis of possibility for growth • Objective assessment of performance by the top • Good way to structure a business portfolio	• Extra management layer between top and business unit • Different course per division • Difficulties in separating task of top, division, and business unit • Difficulties in assessing responsibility for results • Top loses touch with markets • Duplication of staff functions

A condition for the abolition of the divisional layer, or a further decentralization of the business units, is a strong strategic management capacity of the business units. These business units have to be fully equipped to handle their own strategy development. The top operates at a distance and contributes an explicit 'umbrella vision and course'.

Business unit (BU) structure

Figure 4.5 displays an outline of a business unit structure. Such a structure can do justice to responsibility for results, decentralization of authority, and market orientation. In its purest form, a business unit structure requires business units to be fully equipped with their own service departments and, as such, is equal to a structure where a number of subsidiaries operate below a shared top.

However, a business unit structure is not without problems either, as appears from the following quotation: 'For me, the real thing is that I still

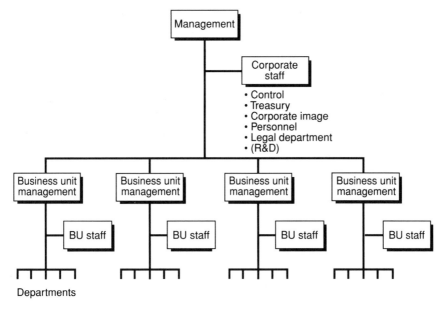

Figure 4.5   Business unit structure

hold the final responsibility. When do I intervene if something threatens to go wrong, and when do I leave well enough alone and stay at a certain distance?'

The business unit structure presupposes a full strategic management capacity of the business units and a limited tendency from the top to assume this role. If a concern wants to concentrate on more product-market combinations, and the role of the concern is limited, a business unit structure is an excellent delayering option.

The business unit concept does enjoy a certain degree of popularity. This does not prevent the fact that we do not often come across a business unit structure in its purest form but, in many cases, a watered down version. While it is not really correct to refer in these cases to a business unit structure; fashion dominates application in a real sense. When we refer to a business unit structure in this book, we always refer to a business unit structure in the real sense.

In Box 4.5 the advantages and disadvantages of a business unit structure are listed

One of the executives we interviewed saw absolutely no problem with autonomy hampering synergy: 'Let the business units compete with each

Box 4.5   Advantages and disadvantages of a business unit structure

Advantages	Disadvantages
● Good opportunity for delegation of responsibility for results	● Separation of central and decentralized authority
● Strategy remains close to the entrepreneurial environment	● Competition for services and attention from the top
● Own responsibility for management of processes	● Autonomy hampers synergy
● Stimulates entrepreneurship	● Top now dependent on business unit managers
● Top can concentrate on strategy and portfolio	● Duplication of staff functions

other, as long as it doesn't result in a price war. If it is real synergy you are looking for, you need to merge and integrate the business units'.

Measures to enhance the effect of a change to the top structure

Organizations which have decided to change their top structure have taken a number of measures to enhance the effect of these changes. Figure 4.6 indicates the areas where the CEO can take action to ensure that the flatter top structure will actually work. These actions are explained in more detail below.

Development of strategic leadership

The top of an organization indicates which activities the concern develops. The business unit management then indicates how it thinks it can achieve the set objectives. The achievement of these objectives does, however, need to be monitored by the top and this requires strategic leadership.

Business unit management also has to develop and implement a strategy for its own business unit. This means that it has to look at the environment the business unit operates in and decide which are its strong points compared to the competitors. John F. Welch, jr., CEO of General Electric, answers the question in *The Harvard Business Review* 'What makes a good manager?' as follows: 'I prefer the term business leader. Good business leaders create a vision, articulate the vision, and relentlessly drive it to competition'.

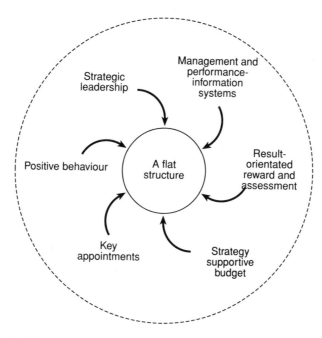

Figure 4.6   Measures for an effective delayering of the top

The strategy which is developed in consultation with the top and its own managers has to be implemented and monitored on the basis of financial and commercial parameters by the business unit management. This places high demands on the managerial qualities of the business unit management. One of the managers interviewed stated that these qualities had to be 'in a person's genes: it is possible to have seven MBAs and still not be a strategic manager'.

Support by means of management and performance information systems

Within flat organizations, decision making is not concentrated in the top. The top does, however, need an insight into the degree to which the individual units achieve their results. This means that criteria need to be developed on the basis of which a company can be run. Apart from the 'umbrella' return on investment (ROI) and other financial criteria, these criteria tend to be organization-specific.

One of the CEOs we spoke to had a thin booklet on his desk. This booklet contained, on one sheet of A4 per business unit, what the performance was for each business unit. He was able to get an insight into performance in a very short space of time. At another organization there was talk of 'once every quarter we all "go in at the deep end", all figures are placed on the table'.

A Dutch survey led to a 'top ten' of criteria, as displayed in Box 4.6.

Box 4.6 Top ten of performance indicators

● Order portfolio	● Productivity
● Delivery reliability	● Accounts receivable
● Motivation indicators	● Degree of capacity utilization
● Work in progress	● Invoicing speed
● Efficiency	● Delivery speed

Every business unit can have its own, unique criteria. These stem from its strategy and the way in which advantages are to be achieved in terms of key success factors and with regard to the competition. By means of a pre-defined system, business unit management periodically reports back to the top, problems are discussed and, where necessary, adjustments are made and corrective action is taken.

In practice, we see that where business units are controlled directly from the top, fewer indicators are used. In one concern, all business units were assessed on the basis of three indicators. The concept was very simple: the business units had to show an improvement for each of the indicators month by month. At another company, a system has been developed which collects data every month from 4,500 profit centres and compares these to budgets and forecasts. The system also allows you to work with the data, you can aggregate and disaggregate results by business segments, countries and companies within countries.

Motivation by means of a result-linked reward and assessment system

In flat organizations, tasks or functions are less important than results. It is therefore important to gain an insight into those factors which motivate business unit managers. It does not do only to discuss what is important; this should also be reflected in rewards. These rewards do not always need to be of a material nature. In many cases, the business unit manager is not in it only for the money. A course at Harvard or INSEAD is often more appreciated than a fat bonus.

In addition to the question 'How do I reward my managers?' the question 'How do I help my managers to develop?' is an important one. In organizations where specialist technical knowledge and experience are decisive factors, there will be fewer managers who have developed strategic leadership skills. We therefore see in a number of situations that organizations wanting to delayer draw in new people from outside. This can only ever be a temporary solution because motivation would otherwise decrease rapidly. Setting up a management development programme which meets the changed requirements of managers and takes account of education as well as prior practical experience is thus very important. Another organization was convinced of the importance of 'own growth'. It had therefore developed a balanced system of spotting management potential and training managers 'on the job'.

Developing a strategy supportive budget

Another important means by which the implementation of strategy in a flat organization can be supported is budget rounds. This is where plans for the available financial means and related performance indicators are drawn up. The business unit management, and not the controller or the financial administration, is responsible for preparing and realizing these plans.

In the budget discussions, the top has to decide which business units need investing in to be able to realize strategy.

Characteristics of these budget rounds are:

- the person responsible for the realization of the budget draws up the budget; the top approves the budget after it is checked and, if necessary, adjusted
- the budget allocation is directly related to the choices of the top regarding group activities, the strategic advantages that have to be maintained or gained with regard to the competition
- if various units want to realize various strategic objectives, resources, people and control take place according to these objectives
- the management layers are directly responsible for the degree to which they manage to realize the agreed competitive advantage and output
- each unit may have different criteria for the allocation and control of the budget.

Key appointments

'The right person in the right place' is essential for a flat organization. This is particularly valid for top management posts. Good co-operation is vital, as the description that one of the executives interviewed gave of *the* most important condition for success testifies: 'a close-knit top team, without weak links'. This means making optimum use of knowledge, skills and personalities. By combining these qualities, management teams are able to achieve the agreed results.

At the *top level*, attention needs to be given to factors which support a successful strategy development and implementation. These are the factors which were described in the model used on page 143 in Figure 4.6 – budget allocation, performance information and control, result-linked assessment and rewards, key appointments, cultural development and structural leadership (of the top). At *business unit level*, managers within flat organizations have to be entrepreneurs, acting as teambuilders.

Delayering of the top can entail difficult decisions regarding appointments and suitability. One of the executives mentioned the following in relation to this: 'The most difficult thing was that a number of people could not handle their new role. We had to decide to let these people go, which is often best for both parties'. The final decision often lies with the person at the top. Honesty and integrity are prerequisites for this.

Positive influencing by means of displaying positive behaviour

In one company, you may see that a strongly developed analytical capacity is appreciated throughout the entire company. In another company, attention is focused on enthusiasm and team spirit. In yet another company, you can see everyone walking down the corridors just that little bit too quickly, as if they are hurried along by somebody.

Culture can be discussed at length, but it is more important that it is reflected in the behaviour of the person at the top. This means, among other things, that the top has to have a feel for culture and is able to indicate what behaviour is desirable and what is not. Negative behaviour is punished and positive behaviour is rewarded. The top may sometimes take deliberate action to positively influence the cultural development.

Within flat organizations, a strong cultural development plays an essential role. Again, the top needs to show the desired positive behaviour. Merely discussing a cultural change as, for instance, a change in focus from role to results, will not work. If the top continues to insist on status, playing political 'games', prescribing rules, and the paper tiger is not chased, cultural change is doomed to failure.

DELAYERING OF MIDDLE MANAGEMENT

The middle management of an organization – all managers below the first line – is responsible for a large range of management tasks. When this middle management becomes too large, the organization becomes bureaucratic. This can lead to blocking of information and the customers will suffer.

In most cases, middle management will have grown slowly but steadily: posts will have been created for certain individuals, new problems will have led to the creation of new departments, far-reaching specialization will have led to new positions being created. After a certain amount of time intervention becomes inevitable.

In our discussion of its delayering, we will first consider the *roles* of middle management. By changing the way in which the company is organized, it is possible to reduce the number of roles. This enables delayering. We will subsequently look at the measures that can be used to ensure the proper functioning of operational processes within a flat organization.

Roles of middle management

At AEGON and Avéro Verzekeringen, management development programmes were important elements in the delayering process because of the realization that changing the way in which the company was organized also required a change in the roles of managers. When these roles are known, we can look at possible ways of organizing which reduce the number of roles. This contributes to the organization becoming flatter and more effective. The most important roles of middle management have been outlined in Box 4.7 (45).

It is important to bear in mind here that managers and staff do not actually add value in the same way an operational worker does. Only employees actually involved in the operational process add value. The only value of managers and staff is that they improve the performance of those employees. Management and their staff are overheads which are only worth having if they actually add value. In order to be able to assess how delayering can be achieved, we have to find substitutes for the roles of middle management. The more alternatives we can find, the more scope there is for delayering.

Box 4.7   Roles of middle management

● Motivating	● Setting goals
● Measuring	● Planning
● Co-ordinating	● Linking communications
● Assigning work	● Training/coaching
● Looking after personnel matters	● Record keeping
● Providing expertise	● Providing leadership

In Box 4.8 are shown the actions which can be taken to substitute the role of the middle management. The most important structural measures are to organize around processes and to work in broad task groups. These structural measures have to be complemented by supporting measures to reinforce the effect of a structural change.

In this matrix we have indicated to what extent a certain measure leads to a reduction in the role of middle management. The measures mentioned are described more fully on the following pages. We do have to bear in mind, though, that these measures can never stand alone. We shall see that none of the measures reduce all roles. This means that a considered combination of measures is required so that all roles of middle management are reduced, and the added value and the performance in total, increase.

We will consider the possibilities to reduce the role of middle management, and so the number of hierarchical levels, but, first, we will look at the way in which tall organizations are generally organized. Following this, we will discuss the two principles that contribute to delayering.

Possibilities to reduce the number of hierarchical levels

The two most important organizational principles managers use when delayering are that they organize their processes around product-market combinations and that they stress the importance of teams.

All of the cases involving delayering of the middle management are concerned with 'reorientation'. The aim is to arrive at groups working as much as possible for one product or market. At DAC, TQMS was introduced to achieve this objective. AEGON and Avéro Verzekeringen developed organizational units in which teams were responsible – and accountable – for an entire process. In all cases it proved possible to reduce

Box 4.8   Options to improve the role of middle management*

Roles of middle management	Structural measures				Supporting measures			
	Organize around processes	Work in broad task groups	Promote internal entrepreneurship	Develop process controlling information systems	Introduce flexible reward structure	Award contracts to suppliers/customers	Change personnel selection and training	Promote behaviour changes
Motivate	X	X		X	X	X	X	X
Measure	X			X				
Co-ordinate	X	X	X	X	X	X	X	X
Assign work		X		X				
Look after personnel matters		X	X				X	
Provide expertise		X		X			X	
Set goals	X	X	X		X	X	X	X
Plan		X		X		X		
Linking communication	X	X	X		X			X
Train		X	X					
Control	X			X	X			
Provide leadership		X	X					

* Compare Lawler (45) on 'Substitutes for Hierarchy'.

the number of layers by changing the way in which the company was organized.

The following quote illustrates very well how the systems that have grown can hinder: 'Our company did not have problems because of a lack of effort . . . Its problems cannot be blamed on an individual or a group. A lot of dedicated people are being eaten alive by a system that is causing these problems. These changes are not an indictment of anyone, but business as usual will not allow us to deal with the challenges of the future. If the system is left as it is, it will break down'.

In many organizations with a large middle management we see that activities are organized around functions. These organizations also tend to have a strong hierarchical structure and policy making and execution of operations are strictly separated. This phenomenon is based on a number of classic organizational principles.

Box 4.9 lists the most important principles used.

The principles mentioned are based on the achievement of maximum efficiency in a situation which can be characterized by a large degree of predictability, limited product differentiation and repetitive actions. Companies which are in this situation might find that these principles are effective in realizing efficiency.

Box 4.9 Principles in hierarchical structures

- All tasks which are necessary to the realization of the organizational objectives have to be divided into highly specialist tasks. Employees need to understand their jobs. Expertise is obtained faster by concentrating on a limited number of tasks.

- Every task has to be carried out according to a consistent system of abstract rules. This enables the manager to reduce uncertainty as a result of individual differences in the way a task is carried out.

- Positions or roles have to fit into a hierarchical structure within which the authority of superiors over subordinates is established.

Changes in factors concerning the business environment, such as a decrease in predictability of demand and a differentiation of demand for products, lead to a decrease in uniformity. The principles mentioned limit flexibility, innovative capacity and customer-orientated action. For this reason they are no longer suitable as a point of departure for the organization of companies.

Within functional structures, traditional reactions to the increased complexity are:

- fighting back the need for control by, for instance, standardizing working methods, stocking up or limiting the assortment
- increasing the need for control by, for instance, increasing the speed of measurement and control cycles, introducing extra checks and increasing the head count to solve specialist management problems.

The effects of these actions vary. They are intended to increase the managerial capacity. A number of these actions lead to the appointment of more managers, to a larger staff or to a limitation of the commercial capacity. Higher costs or lower returns are the consequence. Carrying these actions too far will lead to pathological symptoms (9).

An alternative is to structure the organization around processes and carry out work in teams. A discussion of these principles will follow below.

Organizing around processes instead of functions

Figure 4.7 shows how a product or service is arrived at within a functional organization.

Servicing several product-market combinations leads to complex management, a large degree of co-ordination, long waiting times and stock forming. The point of departure is maximum utilization of capacity of both people and production resources. It is obvious that gearing all these activities to each other and co-ordinating them requires a large management capacity.

Organizing the work around processes (as outlined in Figure 4.8) instead of around functions requires fewer managers. Decisions can be made much faster. Because product-market combinations are at the centre of attention, the decentralized responsibility for results equally increases. This solution may lead to a duplication of expensive or unique capacity, a problem which can be avoided by grouping this capacity into units. Because these units are then involved in the provision of internal services, they become cost centres geared towards efficiency. By means of contract management, co-ordination can take place between profit centres and cost centres. In essence, organizing work around processes allows for the management of these processes to be decentralized and simplified.

Figure 4.9 shows the consecutive steps. In the *original situation*, several product-market combinations are serviced by function-orientated departments. Different products are produced by different functions. A large

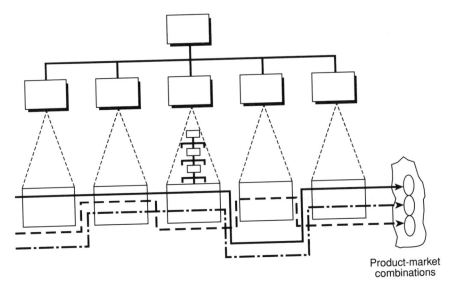

Product-market combinations

Figure 4.7   Complex process streams in a functional organization

internal complexity and a large degree of control and adjustment are the consequence.

The organization has to take the following steps.

- *Separation of primary processes into product-market combinations* By separating the processes and organizing them into product-market combinations the internal complexity, and consequently the need for control and adjustment, decreases.
- *Separation of primary process into process steps* Some primary processes cannot be managed from one point (because the maximum span of control is exceeded) and therefore have to be separated into various steps. This separation (multiplication or horizontal differentiation) gives rise to a new management layer.
- *Combining unique or expensive capacities into cost centres* Where duplication of unique or scarce capacity occurs, combining these capacities is a possibility. This concentration leads to the creation of cost centres.

An important condition for being able to organize work around processes is that the order stream does not fluctuate too much. Should this be the case, then one department can be under utilized whereas another one is over-

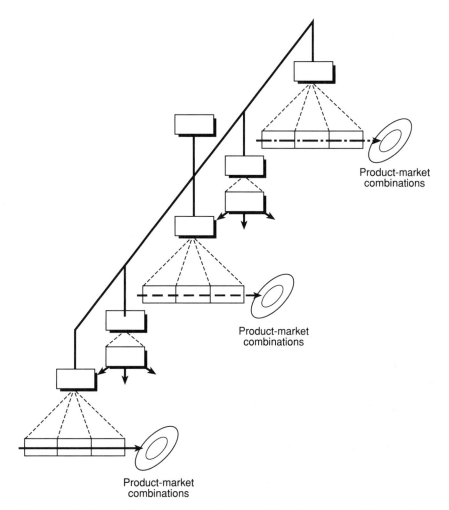

Figure 4.8   Streamlining processes by organizing them around internal or external product-market combinations

occupied. This situation requires further analysis before a decision is made to change the way in which the company is organized (36).

Organization around processes rather than functions leads to a decrease in management complexity. The advantages of this may be an increased responsiveness and an increase in the speed with which market signals are translated into products. By introducing cost centres, loss of efficiency is kept to a minimum.

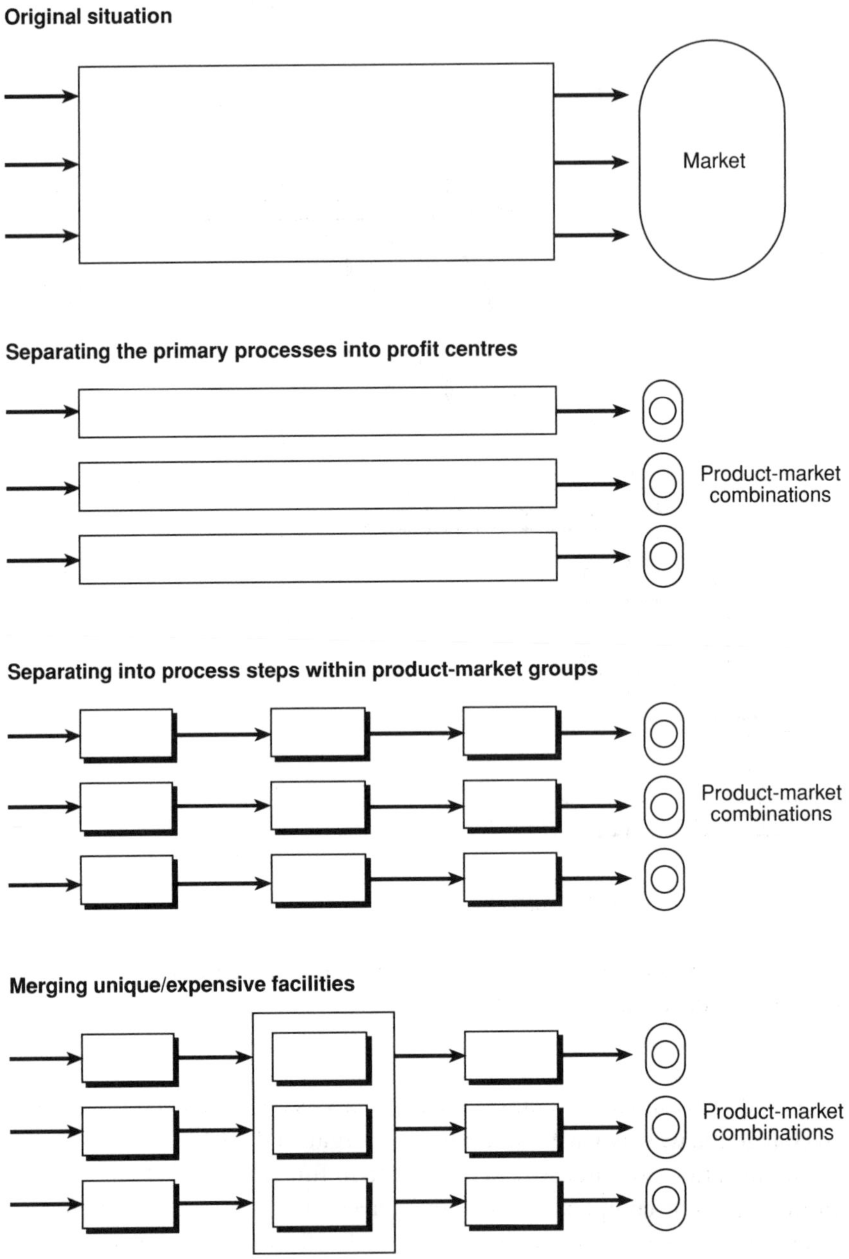
Original situation
Market
Separating the primary processes into profit centres
Product-market combinations
Separating into process steps within product-market groups
Product-market combinations
Merging unique/expensive facilities
Product-market combinations

Figure 4.9 Organizing around processes step by step

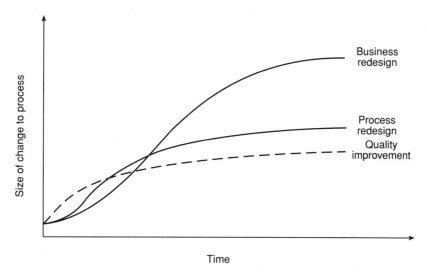

Figure 4.10   Three forms of 'organization around processes'

To organize around processes tends to lead, in a great number of cases, to vast improvements. Business (Process) Redesign is the term now used in many organizations. Redesign involves questioning all existing ways of working, procedures and departmental boundaries. One of the results of Redesign is that companies become flatter.

When taking a closer look at Redesign, we see that it occurs in three different forms (see Figure 4.10). Adjustment of the process is the point of departure for all three forms.

- *Quality improvement* starts with the existing process. It involves a structured, step-by step search for improvements. Despite its good results, this process eventually reaches the point where improvements become more marginal: the law of diminishing returns.
- *Process redesign* only looks at the products to be produced and scrutinizes the ways in which they are produced. All existing methods and procedures are questioned. Information technology plays an important role in the redesign. The results of any changes tend to form the subject of many discussions.
- *Business redesign* This tends to be a predominantly strategic process. The central questions usually are: 'Who is tomorrow's customer?', 'What are the demands of tomorrow's customer?' and 'What are the technologies

which will be available tomorrow?'. Depending on the answers to these questions, the processes are filled in.

On many occasions outrageous goals are set. This last way of organizing around processes can lead to spectacular changes and results. Delayering will almost always occur with Process and Business Redesign. In the case of Quality Improvement, the existing structures are usually maintained.

Working in broad task groups instead of specialized functional departments

Following on from the organization around processes, it is possible to reduce the need for control within a department responsible for (part of) a process. This (part of a) process equally requires co-ordination and control. Separating work into functions within a department requires a large amount of planning and co-ordination at a decentralized level. This disadvantage can be counteracted by creating broad task groups.

The rules of thumb for working with broad task groups are listed in Box 4.10 (1).

Box 4.10   Rules of thumb for broad task groups

- Groups carry out activities as independently as possible. This means that groups must have access to control capacity and have to be involved in planning, support and control activities.

- The members of a group must be able to handle all activities necessary to the process.

- Groups should consist of a minimum of four, and a maximum of 20, people.

- Rewards are largely based on availability for group tasks.

- Within groups the co-ordinating role can be fulfilled by members of the group (in rotation).

One of the managers interviewed commented with regard to the above: 'We faced two great challenges: one external and one internal. The external challenge was to produce high-quality, low-cost products that clearly respond to customer needs in a world of rapidly increasing competition. The internal challenge was to continue to develop the kind of corporate environment which enables this to happen by enlisting the full capabilities of our whole team to achieve continuous improvement in all our activities'.

Working in broad task groups reduces the need for control at a decentralized level so that the number of managers providing leadership to the shop floor is kept to a minimum. Obviously, there is a need for harmonization between these task groups. Ideally, this is taken care of in management teams.

The role of these management teams is as follows:

- ensuring the uniformity of the output of task groups carrying out comparable processes (in the case of multiplication). This means that the customer receives comparable products or services, independent of which task group produces these products or services
- harmonizing the transfer from one group to another (in the case of horizontal differentiation).

Introducing broad task groups may lead to an increase in satisfaction for interested employees.

Measures that increase the effects of structural changes

To enable delayering of middle management, it is not sufficient to take measures aimed at structure alone. In order for the new structure to actually work, action in the areas mentioned in Figure 4.11 can be effective. Below you will find what these measures contain.

Development of intrapreneurship

Organization around processes and in broad task groups leads, in fact, to the formation of elements responsible for their own results. These can then operate as semi-autonomous units within the organization. This means that the responsibility for results of the business unit as a whole can be translated into the results to be achieved per department. Departmental managers and employees thus become intrapreneurs. In many cases it is not necessary to specifically appoint a 'leader' of a broad task group because the person to whom intrapreneurship appeals most will come forward of his or her own accord. This person often also displays the type of positive behaviour which can have a motivating effect on the behaviour of others in the department. Leadership is in the 'genes', as one of the executives already indicated.

Support from process-oriented information systems

The focus in the development of information systems is that these do not only support the execution of a process, but also improve the management

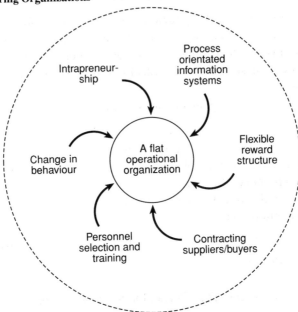

Figure 4.11   Focus points for the effective delayering of middle management

thereof. In addition to this, information technology offers the possibility to disseminate information and make it available at the place of work: distributed data processing, advanced database management systems and means of communication.

Relevant control data are available to managers and employees on the shop floor who can then make decisions based on these data. At one company, unit results were periodically passed on to all staff. It transpired that this had a positive influence on people's involvement in their jobs and, thus, on efficiency.

Many publications in this area advocate the theory that developments in information technology will automatically lead to flatter organizations. Information provision and automation can only ever be supporting means. Managers have to decide for themselves if and how they will use them. The technical possibilities in themselves do not determine whether a company is tall or flat.

Motivation through a flexible reward structure

It is important to translate these new work methods into a flexible reward system, and relate this, for instance, to performance in the newly formed broad task groups and organizing processes around product-market combinations. This can be realized, among other means, by making fringe benefits more flexible. In addition, it is possible to let the results achieved by a business unit filter through in some form (shares, options, bonuses) to those employees whose shows of initiative have led to these results (69).

Direct influence by means of contracting customers/suppliers

In order to organize work around processes, task groups must be able to control input, output and the necessary resources. This involves being able to influence customers and suppliers, inside or outside the company and internal contracting offers an excellent opportunity for this. It allows managers to be assessed on agreements they themselves have made. It also allows for a direct feedback of customer and supplier satisfaction and of returns. This feedback has, provided all agreements are met, a positive effect on motivation, co-ordination and goal setting.

Changing the selection and training of personnel

Training does not only involve specific technical knowledge. Spreading the roles of middle management also leads to a change in general knowledge and skills requirements, such as social skills, meeting techniques, decision-making skills in groups, contracting skills and financial knowledge.

The knowledge and skills required are strongly linked to the tasks a group is supposed to carry out and the way in which they are carried out. When recruiting new employees, it is important to bear in mind whether they will fit in with the group. Attitude is almost as important in this as knowledge. In a number of cases we came across situations where people working in a task group could decide themselves whether others fitted in with their group. There are both advantages and disadvantages to this approach, but it at least it stresses the importance of teamwork.

Supporting changes in behaviour

Common practice, to a large extent, determines the culture within an organization (34). It is expressed in such outward appearances as ways of dressing or choice of car. Similarly, a common (unwritten) norm on quality, customer contact or manners decides the culture to some degree. A strong development of this common practice means that middle management can spend less time on work methods and procedures.

In particular, if, within the organization, there is a strong feeling regarding quality, the role of middle management can change. Because giving meaning to quality is so important, a change of behaviour is necessary in many organizations. 'The bottom line is mentality', as one of the people interviewed commented.

IS DELAYERING WORTH CONSIDERING?

We have seen which measures a number of companies have taken to better organize themselves. A complex set of internal and external causes have led these companies to start a vast programme of change in which delayering was one of the changes.

For managers and executives a number of issues were crucial to the decision to delayer. A ready-made answer to the question 'Is delayering really necessary?' is hard to give. Three of the most important issues in the decision to delayer are outlined in Box 4.11.

Box 4.11   Three important issues for delayering

- Are there dysfunctions in the organization which give rise to a need for change?
- Is management geared towards the changing requirements of the environment?
- Is the added value of each management layer sufficient?

Each issue can be discussed in detail. The way in which companies tackle these issues differs widely. In a number of companies, a group of managers and executives has made an analysis of the changing market in relation to their organization. In a number of other companies, the top person has personally taken the decision to adjust the organization, often despite the advice of an external management consultant more or less to the contrary. In yet another group of organizations, a comparison with other organizations has led to the decision to change. In a few situations, external consultants have been involved in an analysis of the situation and the development of proposals for improvements.

Partly on the basis of considerations of the organizations we studied, a number of questions surrounding the issues of dysfunctions, management and added value have been raised. There is a difference between issues regarding delayering of the top and those relating to delayering of the middle management. It is impossible to come up with a 'digital answer' (in the sense of if more than ten questions are answered with 'yes', delayering is inevitable).

These issues can be used in a meeting of the Management Committee or of management teams concerning the effectiveness of the organization. Answering the questions raised will probably lead to an intensive discussion about the need to delayer. It can also help individual executives in their considerations to adjust the organization.

Considerations for delayering of the top

Several important questions concerning delayering of the top are given in Box 4.12

The questions regarding *internal dysfunctions*, or bottlenecks in the daily functioning of the company, are concerned with subjects which are important to the effective functioning of an organization. Slow decision making, or managerial staff whose tasks overlap can be a reason for change. In addition, it is important for the top to be aware of what is happening in the market and in their line of business and to base its strategic decisions on this. The question is 'To what extent will these decisions actually be implemented?'

Management should be geared towards the ever-increasing environmental dynamism there is in the world. Good management is only possible when there is clarity regarding norms, the budget or the approved plans. Planning is an important matter, but commitment to and assessment on the basis of this planning is at least equally important. It is, after all, very frustrating to be confronted afterwards with different negative results. It is furthermore not effective in a complex and dynamic environment to place the responsibility for returns only with the top.

The remainder of issues is concerned with the *value added* by each layer at the top. Too many layers at the top inevitably leads to an ambiguous separation of tasks, responsibilities and authority. We often see several important-sounding titles among those at the top without it being clear to the outsider or their own managers who does what.

The span of control in the top is closely related to the role of the concern. If that role is one of investor, the span can be quite large. If the role is more a co-ordinating one, then the span tends to be smaller because the work required is much more involved. In the end, the crux of the matter is who is making the real decisions and losing sleep over them and why are the others not?

Box 4.12   Is delayering of the top necessary?

Internal dysfunctions
- Which managers or other key executives have to reach agreement before an important decision can be made and how long does it take for them to reach this agreement?

- To what extent has the top formulated the co-ordination and synergy between units and in what way is this realized?

- To what extent do the tasks of various members of staff overlap?

- To what extent do strategic course changes by the top actually lead to change?

- To what extent is the top in touch with the market?

Management characteristics
- To what extent are responsibilities for planning, approval and realization of business unit results separated?

- To what extent can internal entrepreneurs with a responsibility for results be assessed on the basis of performance information?

- To what extent can the top use the information obtained for the most important focus points (early warning systems)?

- To what extent do business unit managers benefit from (or suffer the consequences of) their results?

- Does the final responsibility for returns lie with the top or are lower levels accountable?

Value added by management layers
- Which top management layers are responsible for strategy and the implementation thereof?

- In what way are the tasks, responsibilities and authority of the top management layers separated?

- Is the span of control in the top in agreement with the role the concern has to fulfil in order to add value?

- To what extent does 'title devaluation' or 'title overlap' occur? (Management committee, daily management, management, deputy manager, general manager, etc.)

- Who makes the decisions in practice and what do the rest do?

Considerations for delayering of middle management

The issues regarding delayering of middle management are outlined in Box 4.13.

Dysfunctions which occur often and which are often a reason to decide to delayer the middle management relate to a strict separation of functions. A separation between policy and execution can also be a reason for delayering, as is too rigid an approach to market potential. These separations can lead to too long a time span for product development. They also limit the possibilities for the development of widely employable managers. Because many problems cannot be solved within one function, they tend to strand in the many forms of consultation, which in itself forms an indication for delayering.

The key word in *management* is making managers at middle management level responsible for results. If this appears to be impossible, delayering could be considered. Responsibility and reporting also have to be in line with results. It is therefore important to have access to internal and external information.

The *value added* by middle management depends largely on the average span of control and the number of management layers. In Chapter 2 we gave some empirical facts from the past. Using these rules of thumb, it is possible to determine how tall an organization is in comparison to other organizations, bearing in mind the tendency towards delayering.

By organizing the work around product-market combinations and into task groups, responsibility for results can be assigned properly. This reduces the differences in competencies.

Additionally, in assessing the added value it is important to determine which decisions managers can make themselves without interference from top management or executive staff. The question that does, however, need to be asked here is what these others know more of or better.

Box 4.13   Is delayering of the middle management necessary?

Internal dysfunctions
- How satisfied are you about the speed of product development on the basis of signals from customers?
- Which executives have to be consulted when making decisions in your sphere of responsibility?
- How many managers possess sufficient knowledge and experience to be able to head a business unit?
- To what extent are policy plans based on opportunities spotted by employees?
- In what way is entrepreneurship stimulated within the company?

Management characteristics
- How widely known is the result that middle management has to achieve and to what extent are these managers assessed on it?
- To what extent does the result concern an integral responsibility for returns (or are managers only responsible for costs)?
- How is the responsibility for results expressed in the reporting cycle?
- In what way is corrective action being taken on the basis of bad results?
- To what extent does management take place on the basis of the available information from customers and from the departments they manage?

Value added by management layers
- How many layers does middle management comprise and how large is the average span of control?
- Which decisions have to be approved or signed off by the next level up without them having any additional knowledge or information on the matter?
- Which topics always form the subject of a competence battle between those in charge?
- How well known are the product-market combinations of your organization and how well is the organization geared to these?
- Which processes are being carried out in task groups?

5

GUIDELINES FOR THE DELAYERING PROCESS

At DAC, delayering started with a shock. The 'shock therapy' also included that of 'massacre Monday', 13 February, 1989, when every one of Douglas' 5,000 managerial and supervisory positions was eliminated. The former occupants of those jobs could apply for just 2,800 newly created posts. The 2,200 who were to lose out would be stripped of their managerial responsibilities, but could apply for other lower level jobs, which would be demotions.

At AEGON, the delayering formed part of a lengthy process that started with the merger between AGO and Ennia in 1983. Initially, integration was the main theme. Subsequently, the company embarked on a programme which looked at costs, returns and service. Following this, a broad management development programme was set up. It was not until 1989 that delayering became part of the picture. 'An evolutionary process with revolutionary shocks' is how one of the managers interviewed described this process. Mr Storm, one of the most important pioneers of the delayering process, has set out his management philosophy in a booklet entitled *Manage With a Smile*.

At Elsevier, following the appointment of P.J. Vinken as the new CEO, it was quickly decided that the organization in which divisions had to play an important role offered insufficient scope for control from the top. This realization was soon followed by the decision to do away with the divisional level.

Following the merger of Asea with Brown Boveri in 1987, things moved very quickly. Speed was emphasized over precision 'because the costs of delay are vastly greater than the costs of an occasional mistake'. Mr Percy Barnevik personally interviewed 400 people, virtually day and night, to help select and motivate people to run the local companies.

Avéro Verzekeringen realized, in a relatively short time, a strategic reorientation, a merger with Centraal Beheer and an adjustment of the top structure, including new appointments. Delayering fitted in nicely with this newly developed managerial philosophy in which the accountability of the newly formed business units had an important place.

All this involved a great many changes in a short time. In order to be able to implement these changes, a programme organization group was set up, led by Mr Jacometti, member of the top management team. The programme organization group had to start up and realize a large number of projects simultaneously. Following the restructuring, the process of delayering within the business units started to take shape. The business unit management, in consultation with the departmental managers, passed accountability further down the line.

From these examples it appears that the delayering process can vary quite drastically. We will not be describing the 'one, best way' to delayer, because it does not exist.

In this chapter we will outline a number of delayering scenarios and list a few points in the delayering process which require special attention. Finally, we will look into the conclusions which can be drawn from the case studies in this book.

IMPLEMENTATION SCENARIOS

In most cases a reduction in the number of layers in middle management is not the first step in a change process, but an almost logical consequence of preceding steps. At AEGON, for instance, delayering was preceded by integration, cost control and management development. At Avéro Verzekeringen restructuring and strategic reorientation were the main themes, before delayering was even considered. At DAC we saw a TQMS programme being put into place.

Where delayering of the top took place, matters were different. In those situations we saw an immediate change of tasks, authority and responsibilities of the management layers at the top, which made delayering the dominant theme. We saw power bases being changed by active intervention from the top.

A large number of external factors play a role in the decision to opt for delayering: how large is the external pressure and what financial buffers exist; what are the consequences for employees and how much support is there for the process; how much experience do top managers have personally and the organization as a whole in implementing changes; what is the history of successes and failures of the top management and how strong is the present team of managers; how powerful is the top management and how powerful are those opposed to change? In addition to this the size of the organization is obviously an important factor. Implementing large-scale changes in a company with 10,000 employees is, of course, much more complex than in a company with only 250 employees. Yet we see that changes in large organizations, such as ABB with 240,000 employees can come about very quickly.

In short, the way in which changes can best be implemented is influenced by a multitude of factors. It is therefore impossible to give one, uniform approach to implementing changes which is applicable in every situation. We can, however, devise a few scenarios for implementation.

In reality we find that the following questions require an answer.

- Does delayering have to be realized gradually or quickly?
- Does delayering have to take place organization-wide or within the individual business units (integral or partial delayering)?

We will first discuss the choice between gradual or rapid delayering and then look at partial and integral scenarios.

Opting for a pace: gradual or rapid

The motivation and perceptions of management do matter in the choice of pace. Another important element is the balance of power: what is the relationship with the Board of Directors or Supervisory Council, how does the Board of Management function internally and how much authority has the top managed to acquire?

It does make a large difference whether the person at the top is motivated by 'the constant improvement of weak spots' or by working as a team to develop and realize set strategies and transferring enthusiasm. Past experiences also play an important role. A top which is used to working in a political environment will choose a very different pace from the top which is used to working in a strongly competitive, action-focused environment. If the person at the top is recruited from outside, his or her perception of management can be very different from that of the organization. This can lead to a culture shock and the realization of a number of changes in a relatively short time. The number of people involved in the changes is also an important factor. This number is usually smaller in the case of delayering at the top than in the case of delayering of middle management.

Below you will find a global outline in which the difference in pace and a number of underlying factors is discussed.

Gradual: heading in the right direction step by step

In the case of a gradual change, the emphasis is usually on a large amount of support for delayering. In this scenario, themes such as 'corporate identity', 'customer service' or 'result orientation' are introduced at regular intervals. When one theme has led to the required results, a next, but related, theme follows; 'Evolutionary, with revolutionary shocks'.

This scenario is characterized by a calm but steady pace. Results really are achieved. A style based on consensus dominates. The top follows and manages the process and often adopts an initiating and enthusing attitude. External pressure does exist, but there is sufficient financial scope for in-depth investment. One of the managers interviewed remarked, 'in the short term an operation of this nature is extremely costly. It should actually take place when things are going well'.

Rapid: a purposeful, 'clean' operation

In the rapid scenario, the person at the top finds him- or herself somewhat out on a limb with the corresponding risk of severance. In the Boardroom plans are developed. Following this, the change process is implemented at high speed with authority playing an important role: 'When employees see the improvement, support will follow automatically'. In this scenario we quite often see people quite high up in the hierarchy falling by the wayside or sometimes temporarily being replaced by interim managers. Because success is required quickly, we often see a process which is predominantly based on performance indicators.

It is extremely difficult to realize this scenario simultaneously within the entire organization. This is why it tends to be implemented 'layer by layer', thus involving three layers: the layer which is subjected to delayering, the layer above, and the layer below. When, for instance, the divisional layer is being eliminated, tasks move to the Board of Management and the business units. These layers have to be able, from the point of quality and capacity, to carry out these tasks.

In many situations, the structure as well as the staffing of these layers is therefore changed. In reality, however, it does take quite some time before the way in which the organization operates truly changes. Rapid delayering can help to gain time, but often not quite as much as was initially expected. In a number of situations it can take up to a year to conclude the first step. Only after this has happened does it become clear that the actual implementation will take much longer. An appropriate quote for this scenario is: 'You can't postpone decisions by studying them to death'.

The size option: partial or integral

The option to delayer either the top or the middle management layer does influence, to a large degree, whether the process is tackled partially or integrally. When delayering the top layer, there is no choice: you either go for it or you do not. What takes place here is changing power bases. The actual choice is for maintaining the divisions or not. Half-hearted solutions seldom lead to optimum results.

When delayering the middle management layer, managers can opt for departmental-, management-, or business unit-specific solutions. For one, management delayering can contribute to an improvement of efficiency; for another, the introduction of, for example, product or account management can give optimum results.

In the following sections we will describe the partial and integral approaches.

Partial: unit after unit after unit

When a company opts for the partial scenario, it prefers the change process to take place business unit after business unit or department after department. Specific situations require a specific approach. Looking at the organization as a whole, it is possible to distinguish separate units or departments on which attention can be focused. After the top structure at ABB started to take shape, we saw a variety of solutions in the various subsidiaries. Success can reflect on subsequent units. In particular, in a situation where there are independent units in which delayering can be more effective than in other units, this scenario can work quite well. In a situation where the units are strongly interrelated or where the group aims at giving a unified image to the outside world this scenario is less suitable.

The scenario relies on a small scale and situation-specific solutions. There is no uniform pace. The individual situation dictates the degree of intervention, from rationalization to gradual approach, more aimed at improving. In this situation, top management can decide for itself whether it wants to take an active role in the change process or remain more in the background.

Integral: everything at once

In particular, when the change process involves the top only, integral solutions are possible. At Akzo, GE and ABB, as well as at NBM-Amstelland and Elsevier, we see, therefore, that the structure and management of the top change for the entire organization. At ABB and Avéro Verzekeringen, a restructuring of the top had an integral character. The consequent delayering of middle management took place unit by unit.

An integral delayering of middle management can occur by means of programme management. In this situation the top has a clear idea of how the organization should function and how this will contribute to the overall efficiency. This is then worked out into a programme and the goal is realized by means of improvement projects, or setting up project groups, work groups and other forms of co-operation. To manage this process, top management may choose to install a steering committee or to appoint a programme manager. Top management is then directly involved either through participation in the steering committee or through the fact that the programme manager reports directly back to them. One of the people involved also stressed the importance of intuition: 'Of course, it doesn't happen that you all of a sudden have a brain wave and clearly see all the steps involved'.

The choices that have to be made can be displayed in a matrix. In Box 5.1 we have positioned all the organizations we studied in such a matrix. We have to stress that this positioning is not based on categories which have received a large amount of support and are open to objectification but on our case studies.

Box 5.1   Positioning of the cases on the basis of pace and size/scale

Pace/scale	Integral	Partial
Fast	NBM-Amstelland Elsevier ABB GE DAC Avéro (top structure)	Avéro (middle management)
Gradual	Akzo (including corporate identity and formation of business units)	AEGON Hoogovens

We can draw the following conclusions from this:

- *Delayering of the top was, in all cases, an integral process* Considering that delayering of the top involves taking a close look at the entire structure of the organization this is not surprising. It is possible, however, to choose between a fast (ABB, GE, NBM-Amstelland, Elsevier) or – in keeping with the entire change process – for a more gradual approach (Akzo). In the case of the latter, the pace is set by political considerations and a careful preparation of the business units for their new role.

- *Delayering of middle management was, in most cases, a partial process* Apparently, it is difficult to adopt an integral approach to the delayering of middle management. In practice it appears that realizing the delayering unit by unit or sector by sector increases the feasibility and measure of control. It is likewise possible in this situation to opt for a fast or a gradual delayering process: 'It is business as usual during remodelling'. The choice depends on the size of the company and whether it is possible to organize quickly or more slowly around processes.

DAC opted for a high tempo and an integral process. The reason for this was the bad starting situation. It was rather a matter of crisis management whereby TQMS was used as a stepping stone and label.

The decision to opt for a fast or gradual delayering process is reserved for top management. Rational factors do not always dominate. One of the people interviewed explained his choice by saying, 'that's what I feel happiest with'. Personal preferences, motivation and experiences, therefore, play an important, maybe even a decisive, role in the choice of how the process will take place.

CHANGE NEVER STOPS

Apart from the options discussed above, a number of other factors play an important role, independently of the choice for a fast or gradual, partial or integral delayering process. These factors are discussed below.

Factors in the process of change

Managers have become more and more aware of the fact that definitive end situations do not exist, but that what takes place is more a continuous process of change in which the factors playing a role change constantly. This process is illustrated in Figure 5.1 (42).

An explanation of each of the factors in the process of change follows. Thereafter we will look at the differences for delayering of the top and the delayering of middle management. We will discuss topics such as strategic readjustment, political adaptation, cultural redevelopment and structural routinization.

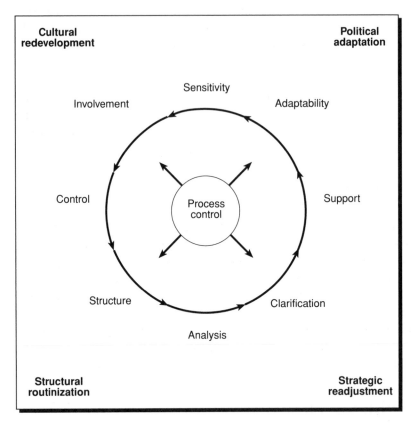

Cultural
redevelopment

Political
adaptation

Sensitivity

Involvement

Adaptability

Control

Process
control

Support

Structure

Clarification

Analysis

Structural
routinization

Strategic
readjustment

Figure 5.1   Change never stops

Strategic readjustment

Organizations wanting to survive have to react constantly to developments in the market. In a number of cases we see that fundamental changes are taking place in a certain line of business which require fundamental decisions. We also notice often that the internal organization is no longer geared towards demands from its environment. In that case a financial and organizational analysis is desirable. A SWOT analysis is often carried out at the same time. Asking fundamental questions regarding operations, control and added value can form a part of this analysis.

In one company a continuous process of strategic orientation may exist. Without drawing up strategic plans, the Board of Management decides, during one of its regular meetings, that it is time for a 'quantum leap'. If the time is ripe and a suitable candidate exists, a decision regarding a takeover or even a merger can be made relatively quickly.

Another company may need the help of a consultancy firm to decide, over a shorter or longer period of time, on a strategic reorientation.

Political adaptation

Making a clear analysis is one thing, communicating the results thereof and clarifying new goals is another and it is at least as important in the matter of being able to actually carry out the changes. Advocates and opponents will group together. For this reason convincing those involved is a prerequisite for being able to implement the changes in the longer term. Ultimately there will always remain a few fervent opponents. The question is, therefore, how much energy to put into the acceptance process? In a number of situations having to let go of inveterate opponents may be inevitable. In DAC mr. Hood stated, 'but there are some klinkers in the middle of the organization, some middle managers, who – because of pushing more authority and accountability down to lower levels – think they are losing their positions and continue to fight it'.

The process of acceptance is, to a large degree, a political process because power and persuasiveness play an important role. In many cases it appears that change is only possible when there is an external threat, internal dissatisfaction *and* an attractive perspective which beckons: 'Under pressure everything becomes liquid', as one of the managers we spoke to commented.

The order for essential changes cannot be simply dealt with in a memo from the top. In order to achieve essential support, it is necessary to reach some form of consensus of opinion and mutual interests, even if this does not appear efficient.

According to one of the managers interviewed, changes which aim to cut out essential functions and lead to a change in power bases do have to be confirmed in writing. This immediately establishes the new posts. It is nevertheless essential to build up sufficient support. It is vital that the management knows it is backed by the Board of Directors or Supervisory Council.

Cultural redevelopments

Starting something new means also leaving something behind. This is an important factor in the considerations regarding existing ways of operating and the implementation of new ways. It needs to be clear why existing behavioural patterns do not fit in with the new goal. In addition to this, the new behavioural patterns have to settle in. This requires a clear image of these patterns. Qualifiers such as 'open', 'honest', 'customer-orientated', 'clear' and 'result-orientated' are necessary, but they need to be given content by examples, otherwise they are merely empty slogans. Furthermore, not *everything* from the past is necessarily bad. Essential values have to be preserved. Showing indifference to employees who formed their values in the past will cause a great deal of opposition. Tackling new things *together* is the best way to realize changes. Co-operation is, in this case, a means to an end and not an end in itself. Co-operation increases the odds of success for the changes.

When this process of cultural development receives insufficient attention, the risk is great that changes to the structure are subversively frustrated; the old behaviour sneaks through the back door into the new structure.

Structural routinization

In the previous chapter we discussed structural adjustment in detail. Delayering is more than the development of a new structure, it is also the implementation and the making operational of this structure. This requires explanations, training, critical surveillance, intervention and assistance.

Figure 5.1 illustrated clearly that an adjustment to the structure is never a goal in itself but always a consequence of other factors. The model makes it appear as if all elements have to run in sequence. This is not the case. The manager in charge of the process has to divide his or her attention over all areas and often operates simultaneously in more than one, hence the fact that the central theme of this model is *process control*. In order to be able to implement changes successfully all four points of focus mentioned require attention.

The model revolves around the process management, the way in which the change process is tackled. Below we will discuss the differences in process management for delayering of the top and the delayering of middle management

Towards a flatter top structure

Delayering of the top is a process which is usually initiated by the Chairman of the Board of Management. He or she may decide to delayer when the distance between the subsidiaries and the top has become too large for the organization to operate effectively and the influence from the top on the direction of the business units has become too restricted.

Box 5.2   Work forms when delayering the top

POINTS OF FOCUS			
Strategic readjustment	*Political adaptation*	*Cultural redevelopment*	*Structural routinization*
Branch/sector analysis	Specialized consultancy	Responsibility for results	Contraction of managerial components
Return analysis	Workshops away from the office	Slogans and new themes	Relocation staff positions
Creating the future	Committed appointments	Sanctioning	Adjustment of reporting lines
Analysis of dysfunctions	Creating coalitions/ lobbing	Appointments on basis of positive behaviour	Setting up committees
Boardroom consulting	Underlining external pressure	Management development	Creation of business units
Analysis of own strengths/ weaknesses	Involving media	Bets	Change in roles and sizes of groups

Indeed, the recipe looks fairly simple. The new structure is the vehicle for far-reaching changes in the power bases which would otherwise not be possible.

In the new structure, the co-ordinating divisional level, which tends to be rather powerful, no longer exists. In reality, this is made possible by offering all, or only a limited number of divisional managers a position on the Board of Management. Through this incentive, resistance is removed and the power bases in the organization are changed instantly. The position of the Chairman of the Board of Management is usually somewhat separate as far as authority is concerned.

The way in which the delayering process is managed is usually determined by the CEO. The following relevant questions are important.

- What has to happen *now* and what can wait till *later*?
- What should I devote *my* time to?
- What can I *delegate*?

A general characterization of this process is 'an intervention in the power bases'.

The problem with this change in power bases is that the rules are drawn up by the players themselves during the game. It is therefore extremely important for the CEO to know that he or she is backed by the Board of Directors. In many cases, the result of the changes in power bases is only known when all appointments are known.

Within a year of the 'definitive appointments', it appears, in a number of situations, that differences of opinion occur at the top and that positions and lines of reporting have to change after all.

As mentioned before, the way in which the delayering process is managed depends on the top man or woman. In Box 5.2 we have outlined a number of work forms which can be applied in order to give shape to each phase of the delayering process.

In the overview, a number of topics and scope for action are given for each phase. In particular in the case of a delayering of the top, the top person largely determines the agenda as far as content, approach and pace are concerned. Through 'Boardroom consulting', the new person at the top asks for advice. Even when convinced of the correct approach, this can serve as a welcome back-up.

Towards a flatter operational organization

The delayering of middle management is usually the consequence of another change. Improving market orientation, increasing flexibility and manageability, improving return or quality are often goals which are directly related to delayering. In many cases delayering takes place naturally during the realization of one of the goals mentioned above.

We also see that in almost every situation where the structure of the organization has changed from a functional one to a product- or market-orientated one, delayering tends to follow soon. After all a structural reorientation means that the company organizes itself around processes and this, in return, reduces the number of management layers. From this point of view, it is very difficult to describe the delayering of middle management as an independent process.

The delayering of middle management, as far as the process management is concerned, does not differ much from other large-scale changes. In general, delayering is part of these changes. Should delayering form part of a change process, then the topics discussed in Chapter 4 all need to be dealt with.

Box 5.3 shows a number of work forms for the delayering of middle management.

Box 5.3   Work forms when delayering middle management

POINTS OF FOCUS			
Strategic readjustment	*Political adaptation*	*Cultural redevelopment*	*Structural routinization*
Analysis of customer orientation

Analysis of flexibility

Analysis of dysfunctions

Analysis of return

Management screening

Assessment of own strength | 'On the soap box'

Set up work groups/ workshops

Development perspective

Communication plan

Preclusion forced redundancies

Underlining external pressure | New themes

Cultural diagnosis

Training

Appointments

Specification of (un)desirable behaviour

Sanctioning (un)desirable behaviour | Process redesign and rearrangement of company procedures

Set up task groups

Programme and project management

Change responsibilities and reporting

Changes in line and staff tasks

Reducing size of middle management |

Because the delayering of middle management is almost always a large-scale process, involving many people, the communication surrounding the change process is of the utmost importance: 'We have spent a great deal of money and energy on internal communication, and yet employees complain that they are not kept informed. I don't understand this', one of the managers interviewed complained.

There are often more questions than answers and this increases the uncertainty for all those involved. While answers are not always available, it is often possible to give an indication of:

- what has already been decided
- what is still being considered
- when decisions are made regarding certain matters 'subject to certain conditions being met'
- who is involved in the decision-making process
- which actions will take place now and in the near future.

By passing on information regarding the order, planning and approach, the uncertainty diminishes. Considering the extreme importance of communication to the delayering process it is advisable to bear this in mind.

MOBILITY AND NEW CAREERS

Delayering apparently leads to fewer career prospects. This is also recognized by M. J. R. Schoemaker and Th. D. Geerdink (69). In their book *Human Talent Management* they discuss mobility and new careers.

In 'traditional' hierarchical organizations, career paths are predominantly determined by the number of levels in the hierarchy. An employee who functions well will rise in time in this hierarchy and his or her function will, therefore, evolve from purely operational to a function containing a number of leadership tasks. The employee's remuneration will increase on the basis of this rise in the hierarchy and/or on the basis of seniority. The problem with this is that employees are sometimes given a job with leadership tasks on the basis of their performance of an operational task, having little or no leadership experience. Training in the skills and instruments of leadership are sadly missing in this type of promotion.

What do career paths look like in the new organizations?

Professionalization and networking of people leads to delayering. In addition to this, professionalization involves employees with a higher standard of education entering the organization. All this means that the career path in the traditional sense changes: the path becomes more level and has fewer steps. In Figure 5.2 the traditional career path is compared with the new path.

Along what lines should we think if 'the hierarchy as career path' diminishes in importance? First of all, we should concentrate on the contributions an employee makes to the organization. These contributions can take many forms. For instance, you could think of contributions in the areas of increasing know-how, improving products/services, accessing new markets, strengthening internal management. In short, a whole variety of subjects which each are relevant to the proper functioning of the organization, can become career paths for employees. This means that career prospects can vary widely between employees, but also that they can be tailored to the needs of the organization.

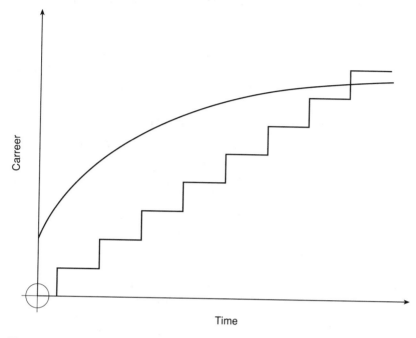

Figure 5.2   Traditional career path and new career development

We are, then, dealing with plural career prospects. The number of different career paths within an organization is largely dependent on the type of organization. In one organization it may be two (in which case the reference 'dual ladder' system is often used), in another it may be as many as four or five. The more complex the functioning of the organization and the more dynamic the tempo of change, the greater the number of career paths there will be.

Career paths based on the mobility model

The essence of outlining the career path of an individual employee can be found in the equilibrium between the requirements of the organization and those of the employee. This equilibrium has several dimensions: the requirements of the function and any changes in those requirements, the abilities of the employee and the development of these abilities.

In an ideal situation, the functional requirements and the employee's abilities are in equilibrium. In practice, functional requirements do change because of changes in the functioning of the organization, and employees do develop their skills.

Changes in the functional requirements and employee development have to be adjusted so that career paths are created, a mobility model is developed. Based on strategic thinking, the employer needs to have an idea as to which functions – for which read career paths – he or she has to offer employees in order to achieve his or her goals.

The mobility model consists of a number of elements.

- *Number of years' experience* This is the number of years' experience an employee has in this or in a related function in another organization. The number of years' experience will thus be more important than the number of years in service (which plays an important role in present career paths). The years' experience indicates the suitability of an employee for a certain type of job and it is possible for this employee to move on.
- *Types of move* In principle, there are four types of move, namely:
  - vertical, to a function at a higher level in the hierarchy
  - horizontal, to a function at the same level in the hierarchy
  - diagonal, a combination of a vertical and horizontal move
  - radial, within a function by a widening or deepening of tasks.
- *Time required to move through the various stages* Here, it concerns the structure of a career as it is envisaged by the employee or as it can be offered to the employee by the organization. The number of stages and the time spent in each stage can vary between types of career. One career might consist of a larger number of stages, or of stages of longer duration, than another.

The above makes it clear that creating career paths within an organization is inextricably linked to the structure of this organization.

Thus, promotion does not only involve 'hierarchical' growth. Figure 5.3 displays new growth possibilities which fit in with a flat organization. In addition to the career paths, the set of instruments used by the Personnel Department will also change.

Box 5.4 shows how the emphasis in the set of Personnel Department instruments needs to shift in order for a flat organization to function properly.

It appears that by developing career paths, it becomes possible to offer a motivating perspective in flatter organizations. Developing these career paths also involves changing the way in which the Personnel Department works.

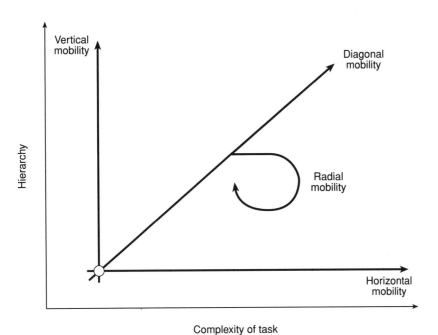

Figure 5.3 Mobility between and within related functions

Box 5.4 Differences between traditional personnel management and human talent management

Personnel management in tall organizations	Personnel management in flat organizations
<ul><li>Vertical mobility</li><li>Singular career path</li><li>Strictly separated/rigid functional structure</li><li>Provide training for specialization</li><li>Assessment on basis of seniority</li><li>Outplacement in case of dysfunctioning</li></ul>	<ul><li>Several forms of mobility</li><li>Plural career paths</li><li>Function 'families'</li><li>Provide training for multiple employability</li><li>Assessment on basis of presentation and potential</li><li>Outplacement as career instrument</li></ul>

CONCLUSIONS

In this section we will look at some of the commonly recommended improvements or conclusions which can be drawn from the cases. All were contributed by those involved in the various companies

Attention given to internal and external communication

Delayering is, in every situation, a drastic process for all those involved. The delayering of middle management involves a change in positions and members of the former middle management may lose out. Most of the companies we researched had created a number of ways (bulletin boards, time set aside for private discussions, etc.) to enhance the understanding of the process. These were not always effective. The fact was that middle management had difficulties imagining what the new situation would be like and was therefore not as accessible as it should have been. 'Soap box sessions' by the top management could be more effective in this transitory phase.

Similarly, in cases where delayering took place at the top, the importance of communication is emphasized. After all, the top structure is under discussion and fast and clear communication with the organization itself and the media is of vital importance. One of the executives commented with regard to this issue, 'Any time you embark on an organizational change of this magnitude, people are starved for communication. You have to talk to them – not only through newsletters and videos, [but] eyeball to eyeball. That's the only way they understand your commitment, and that's what they're looking for'.

Most companies acknowledge the need to handle communication professionally during the delayering process. This fits in with the approach to build communication around 'communication-intensive' moments such as appointments and the introduction of new structures.

Attention paid to culture and management style

Many of the managers interviewed agreed on the fact that changing the existing culture or management style should have been given more time and attention. The so-called 'hard' support measures tended to dominate, thus leaving little time for the 'soft' aspects, such as culture and management style, while progress in these areas could have given valuable support to the 'hard' measures. In one of the companies, the laborious change in culture and management style was attributed to the existing team: '. . . because existing managers took up the new positions, the existing way of working with and relating to each other was maintained'. Some companies tried to get round this problem by recruiting key people from outside.

Attention given to accountability

'The new structure had to give ownership and responsibility. That is what our structuring was all about.' In companies where the middle management was delayered, the realization and facilitation of middle management's responsibility for results at an earlier stage was singled out as an important improvement. Although the decision for a far-reaching responsibility for results was sometimes taken, it was not always backed up with a clear definition of the result and allocation of decentralized budgets. One of the reasons was that the primary process was not yet organized sufficiently for it to be possible to define the result for each new unit. In addition to this, it turned out that the support systems for a middle management with responsibility for results were not ready in time. Without these conditions in place, the implementation of a result-related or flexible reward system proved to be difficult.

Attention paid to human resources

In most cases, delayering runs parallel with the departure of a number of managers or employees. All the organizations we studied considered this a difficult but necessary process. This process required great care, but sometimes the necessary time, funds or support are lacking. The managers interviewed did point out, however, that every departure that was not dealt with properly could have a negative effect on the entire process. In short, management and honesty are desirable in this area.

When delayering middle management, it turned out to be more constructive, in a number of situations, to relocate a number of people internally. This, too, can be done better, for instance by means of a company mobility bureau. Companies have to become aware of the hidden skills of managers and employees and alternative career moves.

For those staying with the company, the flat(ter) structure means that the career ladder, which is traditionally viewed as being tied to the concept of hierarchy, is no longer the same. Flat(ter) organizations tend to ignore the inherent human need for hierarchy. It is therefore reasonable to assume that it is impossible to motivate employees without the traditional promotion perspective.

In contrast to this, the most recent concepts in Human Resource Management (HRM) state that promotion is indeed seen as important, but that recognition of achievements, self-motivation, gaining interesting experience and more challenging tasks and assignments are considered more important.

The vertical ladder, titles, and being boss, move to the background. In addition to vertical promotion, attention needs to be given to horizontal promotion. Horizontal promotion can, in terms of getting ahead, be seen as acquiring new skills, being involved in interesting projects and challenging tasks. These are no longer connected to climbing a vertical ladder

Flatter organizations thus require a completely different HRM approach. When this condition is not met and when the strongly traditional concepts regarding organization, management and control remain the dominant ones, delayering of the organization could be strongly hindered (91).

In the case of delayering of the top, we saw that managers who were not offered a place on the Board of Management will leave in a number of cases. Delayering of the top also involves the more or less forced redundancy of a number of divisional staff. However, it might also be possible to move these people to group or business unit staff departments.

6

DELAYERING INVOLVES MORE THAN JUST LAY-OFFS

At the end of this book we will try to provide you with a 'bird's eye view' of the most important reasons, measures and methods of change related to delayering.

Delayering is a word which sounds simple. When we look more closely at its meaning, though, we discover that there are many dimensions which relate to this development. The most important points of focus are summarized in this final chapter. They have a common theme: 'delayering involves more than just lay-offs'.

DEVELOPMENTS WHICH LEAD TO DELAYERING

From the multitude of developments an organization has to take into account, three touch the core of delayering. These developments constitute the most important reasons for organizations to reduce the distance between the top and the shop floor. They concern competitive pressure, mergers and acquisitions, and the way in which the company is organized.

Delayering: a reaction to competitive pressure

Competitive pressure leads, in many cases, to organizational adjustments. In most lines of business we see this pressure mount rapidly. A good example is the financial services sector: 'In the past the money used to blow in through the cracks under the door; now we have to work extremely hard for it'. In other lines of business the economic climate has equally become more sober. Here, too, there is the desire to be cheaper, better, faster, and so more customer-orientated, than the competitors.

Delayering is seen, in first instance, as an in-depth investment of which the direct profit cannot always be realized in the short term. In the long term it can be expected that the organization starts to operate more cheaply because, relatively speaking, more employees are involved in the primary operational process and overheads are lower. Delayering also releases more energy for entrepreneurship. This has a positive effect on revenue.

In addition to this, an improvement in quality can also be one of the positive consequences of delayering. By making employees responsible for (internal or external) customer contact they are directly confronted with their own mistakes.

Third, delayering can contribute to a faster decision-making process regarding strategic and tactical matters. The time span of the operational process can also be reduced by organizing activities around processes rather than functions.

Flexibility is a fourth possibility to counteract pressure from the competition. Because of their direct contact with the customers, teams are better able to react to the market.

Delayering follows mergers and takeovers

Mergers and acquisitions can, similarly, lead to an improvement in the way in which an organization stands up to pressure from the competition. We are talking here primarily of strategic decisions. After the decision to merge or takeover is made and the legal matters are resolved, the organizational challenge to integrate or co-operate in other ways follows. This can lead, in many situations, to the creation of new management layers. Increased administrative complexity and the limited political room for manoeuvre are partly to blame for this.

In many situations we see that, after a certain amount of time, these extra management layers have insufficient added value as far as the day-to-day management is concerned and in some cases even lead to a decrease in competitive strength. There then follows a reorganization of activities into new units. This reduces the necessary management capacity, which then leads to delayering.

Delayering is changing the way in which you are organized

We also see that within an organization different ideas about the way in which activities are organized raise their heads. In part, because of the increased level of education we see that employees have become more able. One of the managers interviewed commented, 'If you expect people to perform the same task day in, day out, they turn into zombies; and that is exactly what we don't need'. Charlie Chaplin's *Modern Times* are truly gone, 'People do not only have hands, they also have heads'. This means that, at the operational level as well as the management level, it is assumed that people are capable of performing complex tasks with a large degree of independence.

The essence of this development for the way in which activities should be organized is 'organize them around processes rather than functions' and 'work in broad task groups instead of specialist functional departments'. These principles can lead to drastic changes in the ways in which organizations are arranged, which means that the number of management layers required reduces.

DELAYERING INVOLVES MORE THAN THE STRUCTURE ALONE

If we make an overview of the instruments that managers have at their disposal to realize delayering, we see that delayering involves more than an adjustment of the structure. First, it is necessary to create units which are still of a manageable size. A condition of this is a definition of the concept 'responsibility for results'. Furthermore, there are additional measures which reinforce the functioning of a flatter structure: 'We used the new structure as a vehicle for change and had to go back to the processes with fewer people'.

Delayering by reducing the internal complexity

An obvious reaction to the increasing complexity in society and within organizations is to introduce extra managerial capacity. The question is whether this extra management capacity is an adequate reaction: it becomes harder and harder to get a view of the situation, the co-ordination between units becomes more and more complex and the effects that decisions may have become increasingly more difficult to predict. In short, it has become very difficult to keep the ship on course.

In essence, delayering is a different reaction, fighting the increasing complexity by 'cutting the organization up into pieces'. This leads to a simplification of the internal organization. Cutting the organization up into pieces is made possible by creating homogeneous units which operate largely independently and close to the internal or external market.

The top, which is responsible for the concern's strategy and synergy, has to guarantee the advantages of working within a group. The advantages of being 'big and strong' are thus combined with those of being 'small and flexible'. The relative simplicity of the internal organization allows for a better manageability.

Delayering through accountability and visible responsibility for results

In order for the simplification of the internal organization to succeed, it is necessary for each unit, each team, and each employee to be responsible for their own results. Knowing where you stand with each other and addressing people accordingly is a condition of this. Non-compliance with this condition may lead to a fragmentation of actions by the individual units. This could eventually result in the falling apart of a potentially strong concern into unmanageable parts.

Each level within the organization requires a clear definition of tasks, responsibilities and authority, whereby overlap should be kept to a minimum. By backing this definition up with unambiguous criteria, a strong, coherent unit of individual teams can be created. Information systems allow for fast and adequate feedback on performance.

Delayering does not work on its own

Delayering on its own, defined as an adjustment of the structure of an organization whereby the number of management layers is reduced, will fall short of achieving the desired effect. This structural adjustment requires the support of a number of related actions, such as the development of leadership and the recording, measuring and safeguarding of performance. A system of reward and the way in which employees acquire knowledge and experience in various positions also contributes to the realization of delayering. The number of management posts decreases after all, so that other challenges become more important.

Flat structures gain further strength when there are certain agreements regarding performance, for instance in budget rounds. It should also be possible to come to agreement at a decentralized level with internal and external customers and suppliers. Every form of organizing obviously centres eventually on people. The appointments in key positions and the possibilities available to develop within the organization are very important. Similarly, measures concerning appointments and management development can contribute to a flatter organization. Finally, in many organizations wishing to delayer, a change in culture is essential. In order for this change to succeed, the top has to set the example.

A ROUTE TO TAKE

After having described a number of trends and actions we will finally look at the process of delayering. Because this process is rather complex and has a drastic effect on the way in which employees function it requires good management. But even then, it can be a sticky process. The changes do not lead, in the short term, to a fundamental change in the way in which people function within an organization. Finally, it should be realized that delayering is not the end.

Delayering requires good management

Delayering does not happen of its own accord. In order to control the delayering process, proper direction is required. We have seen that there are large differences in the pace and scope of the delayering process. Some organizations tackle the problem 'company wide' while others are more specific. In a number of situations the process evolves at great speed, is very specific and has drastic consequences for employees. In others, the process is more gradual. Attention to strategy, political support and cultural adjustment is important at any rate.

When delayering is required, the top will have to decide on the way in which the process is organized. The style of the leader is often decisive. Making these decisions and acting on them is what we see as managing the process of delayering.

Delayering is a 'sticky' process

Looking at the focus points mentioned earlier, it appears that delayering is not something which can happen overnight. The changes in positions, the appointments and horizontal promotions, and the changes in reporting lines can all be carried out rather quickly. Getting these changes *established* within the organization is another matter. Depending on the size and prior history of the organization we note that it will take at least two to five years before they are actually integrated into common behaviour. In some organizations, an even longer period is not enough to realize the changes in culture necessary for a proper integration of these new ways of functioning.

One of the most important decisions for the top is the decision regarding the pace of the process; gradually and steady, or quickly, accepting that a number of things will go wrong. In particular, in situations were the top has opted to move quickly, expectations are sometimes too high. Again, the style of the leader appears to be decisive for the pace of the process.

Delayering is not the end

We finally come to the subtle differentiation that 'delayering is not the end'. In saying this we mean the following.

First, delayering may well be a fundamental decision, but it is by no means the last. We see that changes around us take place at an ever higher pace. It is vital for organizations to build into the way in which they are organized the ability to react to this environment. Delayering provides an excellent opportunity to increase this ability. Yet, we see that strategic reorientations take place time and again under the guise of 'fine tuning' the organization. This continues until a fundamental change of course transpires, which requires more fundamental adjustments. In addition to this, there is the perpetual pendulum motion between centralization and decentralization. A company's position with regard to these two extremes depends very much on the time and their objectives.

The second meaning refers to the fact that delayering does not always bring universal happiness either. In some situations it pays to abolish the divisional level. A slim divisional level can, however, indeed play a role in promoting the synergy between related units, co-ordination in the area of product development, or co-ordination in market approach. Divisions are not a bad thing *per se*. In other words, it is very well possible that there are organizations which are actually considering, on the basis of a strong need for co-ordination and/or dramatic growth, to establish strategic business units and to link these in with the rest of the organization by means of divisions. These organizations should then also be aware of the latent dysfunctions that this entails.

In those situations where the divisional level has been abolished, the top management needs to take care that the dysfunctions of the old divisional structure do not sneak back in through a gap in the door, for instance by moving people from the former divisional staff to group and business unit level. These people are sometimes quite keen on the old ways and do not hide this. Quite often they sit back to wait and see whether the top will persist on the new route it has taken. Should the top hesitate and leave a power vacuum and/or space for the old role patterns, they will use this to reintroduce the old role patterns. Where this occurs, the top must intervene again some two to three years after the initial delayering process took place to achieve the final scope, role patterns and work culture the concern's staff need. The introduction of former divisional staff at business unit level will have to be justified very clearly by an improvement in the ability to react quickly and an increase in the revenue potential. This requires a very critical attitude towards their 'own' overheads. Should the added value of the transferred divisional staff, by any chance, be found lacking, then this forms a reason for personnel adjustment from the bottom of the organization.

In situations where the dysfunctions have started to dominate, intervention is required. Intervention in the top structure, as a 'vehicle' for change, was considered to be the most appropriate.

At the middle management level it may not be that the maximum removal of layers leads to the greatest increase in efficiency either. In many cases people do need direction. The pressure of the increased responsibility may become too great. Structure after all also offers people security.

In other words, becoming too flat creates its own problems. Finding the optimum situation and handling paradoxes therefore remains the key question for present and future managers.

APPENDIX 1

Delayering in an international perspective

INTRODUCTION

From this book it has already emerged that a flat structure is not the 'one, best way' for every organization. Weber described the bureaucratic model as the most effective configuration for each organization. The fact that Weber was from Germany – that his culture has important similarities to the bureaucratic model – is probably no coincidence.

From the various studies it appears that the culture of a country has a large influence on the way in which things are organized, managed and operate within that country. From the 1960s up to the present day, the theory of and statistical research in the organizational field stems mainly from the United States and Britain. Both countries have a culture which is characterized by a pursuit of individualism and an intolerance of power distances between people. That these countries see the flat organization as the ideal model is no coincidence either and requires attention.

This appendix covers studies in which the relation between the culture of a country and the structure of organizations have been statistically tested. We will also look at a number of comparative structural studies of similar organizations in different countries. Special attention is given to structural studies of Japanese industrial organizations. On the basis of these studies, we will give a characterization of Japanese organizations.

In a time in which the playing pitch of large organizations shifts from international to world-wide, an insight into the cultural differences of various countries and the subsequent preference for a tall or flat structure is of the utmost importance.

CONCEPTUAL FRAMEWORK OF THE INFLUENCE OF CULTURE ON STRUCTURE

G. Hofstede (1980) constructed a conceptual framework for a study of the effects of the national culture on organizations.

By means of a discriminant analysis of a considerable amount of data from various countries, he determined a number of dimensions with which to characterize the cultures in the various countries. These cultural dimensions are:

- power distance
- uncertainty avoidance
- individualism
- masculinity.

The first two dimensions appear to have a large influence on the structure of organizations. An explanation of these dimensions follows.[1] In addition to this, we will go into the positioning and characterization of countries on the cultural dimensions.

Power distance dimension

The power distance is the difference in the extent to which one person can determine someone else's behaviour. A multitude of factors leads to different countries having a different attitude towards power distance in all relations in society (parent and child, teacher and pupil, politician and voter, etc.). This also has an effect on relationships between bosses and employees in work situations and the way in which organizations are structured.

The power distance appears, according to Hofstede, to influence:

- the degree of centralization/decentralization
- the relative number of hierarchical levels in an organization
- the average span of control
- the relation between the number of managers, experts, specialists and subordinates
- the reward structure.

---

[1] The cultural dimensions show a strong resemblance to the structural dimensions developed by the Aston research: hierarchical distance, concentration of power and uncertainty avoidance and structuring of activities.

Globally, it can be said that flat organizations are best suited to countries with a culture in which hierarchical distances are small and vice versa.

Avoidance of uncertainty dimension

Different individuals, organizations and societies, deal differently with the inevitable uncertainties of life. This approach to uncertainties is partially an *irrational process*. Avoidance of uncertainties is largely dependent on the individual and the culture and is expressed in behaviour such as worrying about the future, chauvinism, conservatism, the need for written rules and few changes of employer.

For organizations this means that in countries where people tend to avoid uncertainties to a large extent, there is a greater need for a clear structure, clear procedures and a clear hierarchy, separate from objective factors (such as turbulence in the organization's environment). Organizations in these countries thus tend to have a large (uncertainty reducing) staff and a sizeable middle management layer which informs the top in detail and realizes plans.

Positioning of countries and characterization of the corresponding organization model

Hofstede's study shows a relationship between the culture of a country and the relatively high occurrence of the corresponding organization model (see Figure A1.1). Organizations in the Netherlands, Scandinavian and Anglo-American countries (small power distances, low tendency of uncertainty avoidance), tend to be rather informal and the degree of specialization and formalization is also relatively low. There is relatively little hierarchy, which is reflected in the limited number of layers. The type of organization which corresponds to this is the 'village fair' (implicitly structured) organization.

At the other side of the cultural spectrum we find countries such as Japan, the Latin-American, Islamic and some Asian countries. Organizations in these countries are often characterized by the 'pyramid' (full bureaucracy). The relationships around and between individuals on the one hand and the labour process on the other hand are strictly defined in formal rules, laws or traditions. The hierarchy within the organization is also greatly emphasized.

In countries in south-east Asia (low level of uncertainty avoidance, relatively large power distances), the relationships between people are largely determined by rules, hierarchy and tradition, but the labour process is not strictly structured. The organizational model which dominates in these

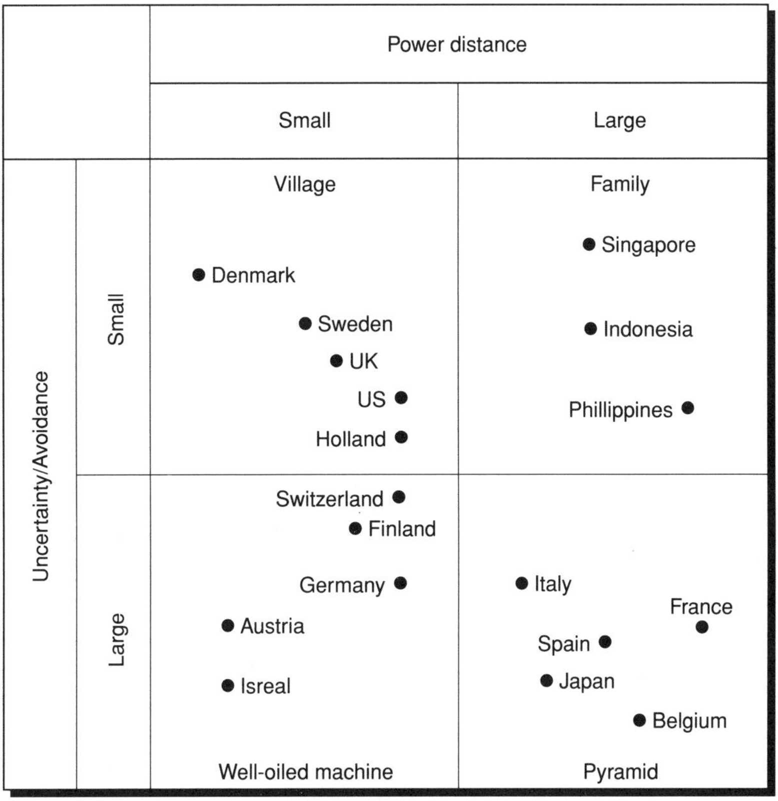

		Power distance	
		Small	Large
Uncertainty/Avoidance	Small	Village ● Denmark ● Sweden ● UK US ● Holland ●	Family ● Singapore ● Indonesia Phillippines ●
	Large	Switzerland ● ● Finland Germany ● ● Austria ● Isreal Well-oiled machine	● Italy France ● Spain ● ● Japan ● Belgium Pyramid

Figure A1.1   Relationship between power distance and uncertainty-avoidance (Hofstede)

countries can be compared to a 'family' (personnel bureaucracy).

In Germanic countries, Finland and Israel the labour process is strictly structured and the degree of hierarchy and formalization of relationships between people is relatively small (in Germany it is often the group or the team that has central authority). The organizational structure which can be found relatively often in these countries is that of a 'well-oiled machine' (workflow bureaucracy).

Comparing France and Germany with the Anglo-American and Scandinavian countries and the Netherlands reveals striking differences. In comparison to the latter countries, power distances in the French culture appear to be very large. This is expressed in a great number of layers within organizations and a sizeable and powerful *cadre*. The hierarchical distances in the Germanic culture do not differ much from those in the Anglo-American and Scandinavian countries. There is, however, a strong need for rules and procedures to avoid uncertainties (the well-oiled machine or bureaucracy).

National comparative structural studies

F. Trompenaars (1990) made an empirical study of the relationships between the nationality and hierarchy of organizations in various countries. In his study, he questioned people in a number of countries about their subjective view on the hierarchical length of the organization in which they worked. The results are portrayed in Table A1.1.

Table A1.1   Characterization by managers from various countries of the hierarchical length of the organization by means of a triangle (Trompenaars, 1990)

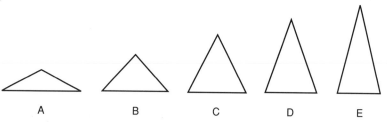

Origin	A & B(%)	C(%)	D & E(%)
Sweden	50	20	30
USA	47	39	14
UK	46	24	25
BRD	41	50	9
NL	41	35	21
Singapore	24	30	46
France	22	43	35
Greece	21	51	28
Italy	15	65	20
Spain	11	43	46
Venezuela	9	44	47

The results show great similarities with those of Hofstede's study. The cultural dimension which, according to Hofstede, influences the degree of hierarchy and the hierarchical length of organizations is the power distance dimension. The score of the various countries in this dimension according to Hofstede's study is reflected in Table A1.2.

While not using any 'hard' criteria, such as the average span of control or the number of hierarchical levels, it is remarkable to see that the hierarchical length of an organization very much depends on the national culture.

Table A1.2   Scores of various countries for power distance according to Hofstede's study

Origin	PDI (Power Distance Index)
Sweden	31
UK	35
BRD	35
NL	38
USA	40
Italy	50
Spain	57
Greece	60
France	68
Venezuela	81

The relationships between culture and organizational structure described above are confirmed by a number of other comparative studies, for example:

• France and Germany (M. Brossard and M. Maurice)
• France, Germany and the UK (J.H. Horovitz; M. Crozier)
• the US and the UK (J.H.K. Inkson, *et al.*, M. Haire, E.E. Ghiselli and L. W. Porter)
• the US and India (A.B. Neghandhi and S.B. Prasad)
• Latin-American countries (W.F. Whyte).

Whyte's study (1969) shows that in Latin-American countries there are vast social differences between 'white collars' and 'blue collars' which, from a structural point of view, is expressed in a large vertical differentiation and big differences in remuneration.

A.R. Neghandhi and S.B. Prasad (1971) observed a difference in hierarchical levels between comparable American and Indian companies in India. The American companies comprised significantly fewer layers than the Indian companies. This is remarkable because it shows that a company does not always have to comply with the culture of the country, but is able to influence this contingency factor by its own strong organizational culture or by the selection and training of employees.

M. Haire, E.E. Ghiselli and L.W. Porter discovered in 1968 that the attitudes and ways of problem solving of British and American managers showed strong similarities. This is confirmed in a study by J.H.K. Inkson, *et al.* (1970). The latter also demonstrates strong similarities between the structure of comparable organizations from both countries, which confirms Hofstede's Anglo-American classification.

J.H. Horovitz's study (1978) shows that French and German top managers (high level of uncertainty avoidance) want to be informed in more detail about their businesses than their British colleagues. There is also more formalization.

M. Crozier had discovered already in 1964 that French organizations are characterized by a higher than average degree of centralization and formalization. He also states that 'the processes of social control that appear in bureaucratic organizations are not uniform and are, in fact, closely associated with the values and models of social relations characteristics of each society'.

M. Brossard and M. Maurice (1974) presented a study which compares industrial organizations from France (large power distance) and Germany (small power distance). The French organizations comprised, on average, five organizational levels compared to three for the German organization. The ratio of 'managers and specialists to the total number of employees' was 26 per cent for the French organizations and 16 per cent for the German companies.

Finally, the difference in remuneration of the highest and lowest paid employee was many times greater in French companies than in the German ones. Employees at the lower level in German companies were far better paid and trained.

A CLOSER LOOK AT JAPAN

It is clear that the Japanese culture is very different to those in Anglo-American and Scandinavian countries. For a better understanding of the Japanese culture we shall look at the following characteristics.

Striking characteristics of the Japanese culture

The most obvious characteristics are the strong group orientation and the corresponding relative homogeneity. This can be explained on the basis of a number of uniform institutional forces. For instance, politics has always been very centralized and integrated into everyday and business life. The *Kaishas* (large companies) are part of large integrated networks of financial institutions, suppliers, universities and the Ministry of Economic Affairs (MITI).

Another characteristic is the great importance of hierarchy, based on seniority, status or position, in personal relationships. In Hofstede's study, this is illustrated by the high PDI score.

As a final characteristic, we list the 'lifetime employment' of the greater part of the professional population. This is due to the *Nenko* system Japanese firms use in their personnel policies. In exchange for loyalty to and identification with the organization, this system guarantees a job for life, and promotion and remuneration according to the number of service years.

These and many other unique characteristics are often used to explain the success of Japanese firms. However, little empirical research has been done into the structural differences between Japanese and other organizations. This lack of empirical data, the difference in culture and the success are probably the reasons why the image of Japanese companies does not quite agree with the reality. There are, for instance, publications which claim that the Japanese organization is the example for the flat organization, with 'lean structures and few management layers' (J. Child, 1984).

Below follows a description of the structural characteristics of Japanese organizations on the basis of empirical studies.

Characterization of the structure of Japanese organizations

As far as vertical differentiation is concerned, it appears from a number of studies (M.Y. Yoshino, 1968; R.P. Dore, 1973; K. Azumi and C. McMillan, 1981; J.R. Lincoln, *et al.*) that Japanese organization have many more layers than their British or American counterparts. An extensive study by Lincoln, *et al.* (1968) shows that Japanese companies had, on average, one and a half organizational levels more than their American counterparts (average of five). Some researchers, such as Azumi and McMillan (1981), came across even greater differences. The management's span of control is relatively low, as appears from the studies mentioned earlier.

Looking at these structural dimensions, Japanese companies have a greater hierarchical length and could logically be expected to have a relatively large number of managers. The personnel structure shows, however, that there is no difference in *management intensity*. The organizations may consist of more levels, but the number of managers per level is smaller. What we see here is a very gradual hierarchy with fewer managers per level (see J.R. Lincoln and Kalleberg, 1985).

A remarkable difference is the great many subgroups in Japanese companies, departments (*bu*), for instance, tend to consist of sections (*ka*), subsections (*kakari*), and teams (*han*).

These subgroups are relatively autonomous and have a great involvement in the decision-making process. *Nemawashi* (consultation in order to arrive at a consensus) and ringi-seido (circulating formal documentation for completion and approval) are instruments which are frequently used. On first sight, Japanese organizations appear to be more centralized, but in reality they involve a greater number of subgroups in the decision-making process which results in a greater degree of decentralization and participation.

These studies show that the Japanese organizational structure is flat in some respects and very tall in others. This is illustrated in Figure A1.2.

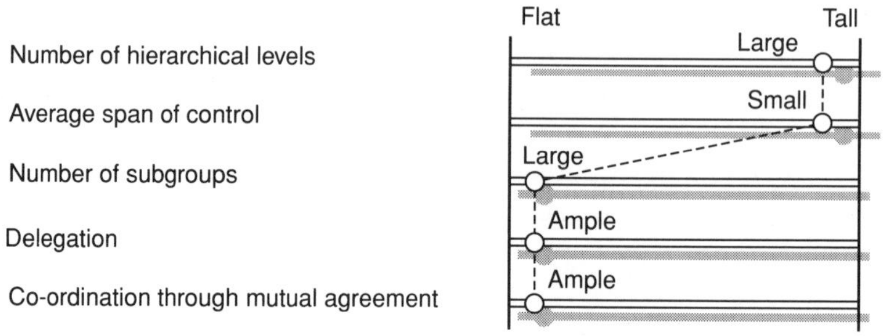

Figure A1.2   Profile of the Japanese organizational structure

This shows that it is very possible for an organization to comprise flat as well as tall elements. The success of Japanese organizations is probably related to the fact that this unique mixture of structural characteristics corresponds so very well to the cultural characteristics, c.q. contingencies, mentioned earlier. First, the large number of layers agrees with the large degree of hierarchy and power distances in Japanese culture. Second, it offers lifetime employment to a professional population, which is inclined to reduce uncertainty. On the other hand, the large amount of delegation to the many sub units (group culture) enables companies to remain innovative and responsive.

CONCLUSION

The national culture influences not only the way in which a company functions, but also the way in which it is organized. This is why Anglo-American, Scandinavian, and Dutch organizations tend to prefer a flat organizational structure. Organizations in, for instance, Japan, Latin American, Islamic and some Asian countries tend to prefer a taller structure.

The organization reproduces, as it were, the social ordering as it appears in the external environment. Contextual factors do, however, retain their influence on the structure of organizations.[2] In a given culture where organizations tend to have few layers, larger organizations will, therefore, have more layers than smaller organizations.

Research into Japanese organizations shows that a mixture of tall and flat characteristics can occur within the same organizations. The mixture depends on the various factors in the culture of countries, such as the degree of power distance, avoidance of uncertainty and group orientation.

Multinational organizations will have to be aware of the cultural effect. The question is how effective an organization which does not take this contingency factor into account can be. This organization will, in any case, have to expend a great deal of effort on the development of its own company culture and the selection and training of personnel.

---

[2] The Aston studies show that a number of contextual factors, such as size, technological dependence on other organizations, ownership structures, etc., influence the structure of organizations (D.S. Pugh, *et al.* 1969).

APPENDIX 2

Research into the effectiveness of tall and flat structures

INTRODUCTION

Up until 1950, it was thought that a tall organizational structure (Weber's bureaucratic model) was the best one. It was J.C. Worthy who broke away from this idea and proclaimed the exact opposite. In 1950 he concluded as follows: 'Flatter, less complex structures, with a maximum of administrative decentralization, tend to create a potential for improved attitudes, more effective supervision and greater individual responsibility and initiative of the employees'. Worthy was also convinced that one, single structural configuration would be superior in all situations. However, he based this theory on his experiences within one company.

Being able to make firm judgements on the effectiveness of flat and tall structures requires more than intuition or the analysis of one single company. Empirical and experimental research into the effectiveness of structural configurations under varying circumstances is the appropriate method.

A study of the literature on the subject (which forms the basis of this appendix) discusses most of the available results of research into the relationship between the length of a structure's hierarchy and its effectiveness. For this appendix we have made a selection on the basis of the following three criteria:

1 the study concerned is a field study of profit organizations or an experimental study
2 in the study, the variable 'length of the organization's hierarchy' is used to define the following:
   - the number of hierarchical levels, or
   - the (average) span of control

3 in the study the variable 'effectiveness' is used to define the following:
   – the satisfaction of the employees
   – the performance (of the members of the organization and the organization in its entirety).

The next two sections give a brief characterization of the studies selected, differentiating between studies concerned with the relation between length of hierarchy and satisfaction and those concerned with the relation between length of hierarchy and performance.

LENGTH OF HIERARCHY AND SATISFACTION

In this section, the studies into the relationship between the level of satisfaction (or, more specifically, the level of needs fulfilment) of management and employees and the structure of the organization are discussed. Table A2.1 gives an overview of the articles in this study.

Management

L. Meltzer and J. Salter (1962) did not manage to find a significant relationship between the length of hierarchy of an organization and the satisfaction of its management. Worthy's hypotheses have thus not been confirmed by this study. It should be pointed out, though, that Meltzer and Salter did concentrate on smaller organizations, which means that it is impossible to draw any conclusions for medium-sized and large companies.

L.W. Porter and E.E. Lawler's study from 1964 shows that the size of the organization is a relevant factor in the degree of satisfaction in tall and flat organizations. In organizations with fewer than 5,000 employees, the satisfaction of the management was greatest when the organization was flat. In organizations with more than 5,000 employees, on the other hand, satisfaction appeared greatest when the organizational structure was tall. There also appeared to be a difference in the satisfaction of needs. Tall organizations did tend to meet needs such as self-development.

The results from E.E. Ghiselli and D.A. Johnson's study (1970) confirm the relationship found by Porter and Lawler between the needs satisfaction of managers and the length of hierarchy of the organization.

Ghiselli and Johnson further demonstrated a positive relationship between the degree to which the 'higher' needs such as autonomy and self-development, were met and the success of the manager. A similar relationship was not found in tall organizations (see also Figure A2.1).

Table A2.1 Overview of studies into the length of the structure's hierarchy in relation to satisfaction

Structural dimensions and type of employee	Highest level of satisfaction			
	Flat	Tall	Other	Study
Relationship between number of hierarchical levels and average span of control:				
– management	X			Worthy (1950)
			X	Melzer and Salter (1962)[1]
			X	Porter and Lawler (1964)[2]
			X	Ghiselli and Johnson (1970)[3]
			X	O'Connell, et al. (1976)[4]
– higher management		X		El Salmi and Cummings (1968)
– lower management	X			El Salmi and Cummings (1968)
– employees	X			Invancevich and Donnelly (1975)
	X			Gannon and Paine (1974)

[1] No relation

[2] Size of organization < 5,000: high level of satisfaction in a flat structure; size > 5,000 *idem* in tall structure

[3] Other needs fulfilment and promotion mechanisms

[4] Large degree of uncertainty of external environment: flat structure, more satisfaction, small degree of uncertainty, tall structure more satisfaction

In summary, we can conclude that flat organizations, as Worthy had already indicated in 1950, stimulate individuality and related needs such as autonomy and self-development. The corresponding behaviour is rewarded with promotion.

Remarkable are the results from the experimental study by M.J. O'Connell, *et al.* (1976). In a simulation of a military conflict, they studied the influence of the structure of the decision group on the types of tension felt in people of that group, under varying conditions of external information. In total, 48 groups of three people were studied. One half of those groups was loosely structured (what we would refer to as 'flat') and the other half was tightly structured (what we would refer to as 'tall'). In the loosely structured groups, people had to treat each other as colleagues, allocate tasks themselves and have a decision-making process on the basis of consensus. In the tightly structured groups, there was one leader, tasks were

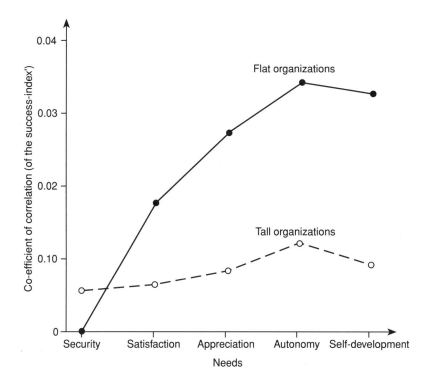

Figure A2.1   Relationship between needs satisfaction and managers' success in flat and tall organizations (free interpretation from Ghiselli and Johnson, 1970)

strictly allocated (by specialism) and the leader was authorized to make decisions on the basis of the data processing of the subordinates.

The external information varied in quantity and specificity. This meant that the groups had to make decisions under different conditions of external information. The study looked at the effects of the various situations on the tensions felt in loosely and tightly structured groups. The members of the tightly structured, bureaucratic groups tended to suffer less from tensions caused by ambiguity and too much work.

When the specificity of the external information was low, the members of the loosely structured group suffered less from tensions resulting from a lack of adequate information. The opposite was true when the external information was highly specific. This is reflected in Figure A2.2.

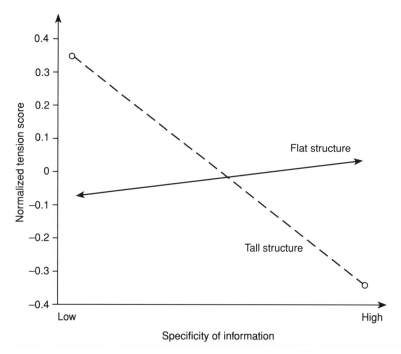

Figure A2.2   Relationship between specificity of information and the tension felt in members of flat and tall groups (free interpretation from O'Connell, *et al.*)

A possible explanation for the latter phenomenon is that highly specific information made members of the loosely structured groups realize that the environment was very complex and, because they participated in the decision-making process, they felt a need for more information. The tightly structured group members did not feel this need.

Higher and lower management

In contrast to previous studies in which the needs fulfilment of the entire management in the various types of organization were studied, A.M. El Salmi and L.L. Cummings (1968) make distinctions on the basis of the level of management. They distinguish between three types of organization and two levels of management: a tall, a medium and a flat organization, and the highest and lowest level of management. From their research, it appears that the management at the highest level in the tall organization gets more satisfaction than that in the medium or flat organization. For the lowest level of management, the opposite is true; satisfaction is highest in flat and medium organizations and lowest in tall ones. They furthermore observed, in tall as well as flat organizations, a positive relationship between the level of a manager's hierarchical position and the level of satisfaction. This would explain the higher level of satisfaction of the top management in tall organizations.

Employees not belonging to the management

The effects of a tall or a flat structure on the level of satisfaction of employees which do not form part of management have been the subject of two studies: J.M. Ivancevich and J.H. Donnelly and M.J. Gannon and F.T. Paine.

Ivancevich and Donnelly (1975) have studied, amongst other things, the differences in satisfaction, stress and anxiety of employees in tall and flat organizations. The results of the study led to the conclusion that employees in flat organizations see more of a fulfilment of their need for autonomy and self-development than those in tall organizations. These employees also tend to suffer less from psychological stress and anxiety.

The following comments should be made with regard to this study:

- the sample may have consisted of only 295 people, but they came from three organizations with very different characteristics and the chance that the characteristics of the organization influenced the results, is rather large
- all employees studied were salespeople. A study (F. Trompenaars, 1990) shows that this professional discipline has a preference for little hierarchy.

Gannon and Paine (1974) studied the differences in attitudes between employees that occurred as a result of far-reaching vertical differentiation. The starting point in this was the effect of maintaining, c.q. breaking, the 'unity of command'. In the complex, tall organization, employees often report to two or more superiors, according to the study. This is in contrast to the flat organization, where employees generally report to one boss. The employees reporting to one boss indicate that:

- selection of personnel takes place on the basis of expertise
- they suffer relatively little role conflict and job pressure
- they experience less need for co-ordination
- the responsibility and autonomy is more adequate.

LENGTH OF HIERARCHY AND PERFORMANCE

In this section, we will discuss those studies which look at the relationship between the length of hierarchy of an organization and the performance. Table A2.2 gives an overview.

Woodward (1968) has been able to show a link between the span of control of management at the lowest level, the type of technology and the performance of the organization. For each class of technology used, ranging from simple to medium and complex, the optimum span of control for production bosses was determined.[1] In companies which were less profitable, this span of control was larger or smaller than the optimum.

Table A2.2 Overview of the studies into the length of hierarchy of the structure in relation to performance

Performance				
Structural dimensions	Flat	Tall	Other	Study
Span of control of lower management			X	Woodward (1965)[1]
Relationship between hierarchical levels and average span of control:				
– management		X		Melzer and Salter (1962)
		X		Carzo and Yanouzas[2]
– employees	X			Farris (1969)
	X			Ivancevich and Donnelly (1975)

[1] Curvilinear relation
[2] Concerns experiment with students

The relationship between the type of technology and the optimum span of control appeared to be a curvilinear relation: a simple technology gave an optimum span of control of 23, an average complex technology 49, and a complex technology 13 employees (see Figure A2.3.) The span of control of the top manager did not appear to be linked to the performance or the technology.

---

[1] This optimum span of control (the span of control in companies with a higher than average performance) agreed with the average span of control in the groups.

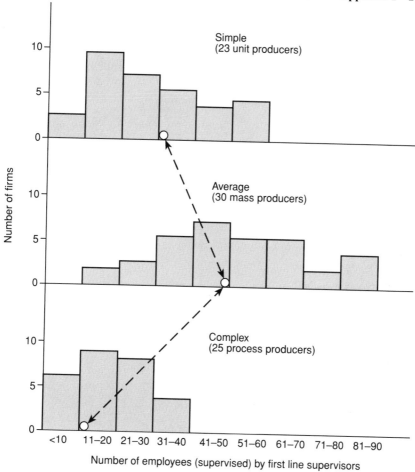

Figure A2.3   *Optimum span of control of production managers in a variety of technological organizations* (free interpretation from Woodward, 1965)

L. Meltzer and J. Salter (1962) have found a positive link between the length of hierarchy of an organization and the performance in 'large' organizations. Among the large organizations, the tall ones were the most productive. Among the small organizations, no difference in performance was found between tall and flat organizations. As we mentioned earlier, the companies studied were very small (the classification was <20, 20–50, >50 employees), which makes it difficult to draw general conclusions.

R. Carzo, jr., and J.N. Yanouzas (1969) set up an experiment to study the effect of the length of hierarchy of the structure on performance. The study consisted of a laboratory experiment in which tall-structured (four levels) and flat-structured groups (two levels) had to solve problems. The results are displayed in Figure A2.4.

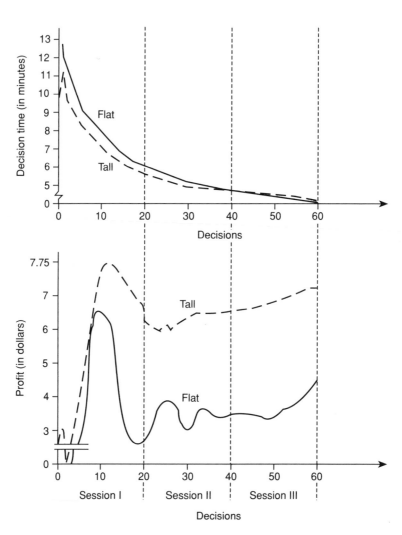

Figure A2.4   Cumulative decision time and profit for flat and tall structures (free from Carzo and Yanouzas, 1969)

There was no significant difference in the total decision time. In the tall structure, relatively more time was lost on hierarchy because the decision had to pass through the various levels. This contrasts with larger amounts of time required by the flat-structured group for discussion, conflict solving and co-ordination.

People in tall structures did perform considerably better compared to those in flat structures. The researchers reckon that this is due to the fact that the decision-making process in tall organizations is of a better quality because of the re-evaluation of the decisions that takes place at the various levels. E. Jaques (1990) recognizes this phenomenon and states: 'We don't need flat organizations. We need layers of accountability and skill'. In his article 'In Praise of Hierarchy' (39) he claims that in many organizations, the hierarchy is dysfunctional and this, he says, is the result of a misunderstanding of the concept of hierarchy.

The nature of the tasks an organization needs to perform requires an hierarchy of several levels of work, the 'span of discretion', and responsibility. An organization in which work is hierarchically ordered by duration and complexity and to which the necessary responsibility is hierarchically linked, will be effective.

A tall structure which is dysfunctional and in which, for instance, management layers are removed to make the organization more effective, runs the risk of frustrating the decision-making process and the functioning of the organization if this is not given proper consideration (see also R.E. Nelson, 1988).

G.F. Farris (1969) conducted a longitudinal study in which he discovered a positive link between the span of control and the individual performance of 151 engineers. In the flat organization, where the average span of control of the management is relatively large, the performance of the employees was better (i.e., they produced more). A positive link exists between the span of control and all performance criteria, number of patents, number of technical reports and assessment of superiors.

In their study into the differences between satisfaction and performance of salespeople in flat and tall organizations, J.M. Ivancevich and J.H. Donnelly (1975) have demonstrated a negative link between the length of hierarchy of an organization and the performance. The salespeople in flat organizations performed considerably better.

CONCLUSION

This appendix has described a number of studies into the relationship between the length of hierarchy of the organizational structure and its effectiveness. The results of these studies do not allow us to draw the conclusion that a flat structure is, by definition, more effective than a tall structure. It is, however, possible to draw conclusions for a number of elements of the problem regarding the link between length of hierarchy and effectiveness.

1 The idea that the level of satisfaction of members of an organization is higher in organizations with a flat structure appears to be confirmed in the studies. This seems to apply, in particular, to managers at lower levels and to employees with a 'borderline function', such as salespeople. Unfortunately, no research has been done into the satisfaction of, for instance, production employees in tall and flat organizations. At the highest level, tall organizations appear to provide most satisfaction.

2 The effectiveness of flat structures is dependent on the situation. Flat structures are more effective than tall structures in a turbulent environment which is complex and constantly subject to change. In contrast, tall structures are better in a stable environment when information is clear.[2]

3 Effective decision making requires a certain measure of hierarchy. This appeared, amongst others, from the experimental study by Carzo and Yanouzas. The organizations with a relatively high number of hierarchical levels performed better than their counterparts. The quality of the decision-making process in tall organizations was higher, because decisions were re-evaluated at various levels.

---

[2] Although the environment becomes more and more turbulent for most organizations, Ansoff (1984) thinks that the external environment of an organization can fall back to a lower level of turbulence because of the introduction of, for example, industrial standards.

BIBLIOGRAPHY

1 Amelsvoort, P. van., 1992, *Het vergroten van de bestuurbaarheid van produktie-organisaties*, ST-GROEP, Oss.

2 Applegate, L.M., J.I. Cash jun., and D. Quinn Mills, November–December 1988, 'Information Technology and Tomorrow's Manager', in, *Harvard Business Review*, pp.128–36.

3 Bachman, J.C., J.A. Slesinger and C.G. Smith, 1966, 'Control, Performance, and Satisfaction: an Analysis of Structural and Individual Effects', in, *Journal of Personality and Social Psychology*, 4, 2, pp. 127–136.

4 Berger, C.J. and L.L. Cummings, 1979, 'Organizational Structure, Attitudes, and Behaviours', in, *Research in Organizational Behaviour*, 1, pp. 169–208.

5 Besselaar van den, P. and Z. Berdowski, Summer 1990, 'Niet meer werk door informatietechnologie alleen', in, *Informatie en Informatiebeleid*, 2, p. 20.

6 Bolwijn, P.T. and T. Kumpe, 1992, *Marktgericht ondernemen, management van continuiteit en vernieuwing*, Van Gorcum, Assen.

7 Brooke, M.Z., 1984, *Centralization and Autonomy: A study in organization behaviour*, Holt, Rinehart and Winston, London.

8 Brossard, M., and M. Maurice, 1976, 'Is There a Universal Model of Organization Structure?', in, *International Studies of Management and Organization*, 6, 3, pp. 11–45.

9 Bums, T., and G.M. Stalker, 1971, *The Management of Innovation*, Tavistock Publications, London.

10 Buyse, J., B. Fruytier and P. van Amelsvoort, 13 April 1990, 'De menselijke organisatie', in, *Intermediair*, 26, 15, pp. 29–33.

11 Carlyle, R., February 1990, 'The Tomorrow Organization', in, *Datamotion*, pp. 22–29.

12 Carzo, R., jun., and J. N. Yanouzas, 1969, 'Effects of Flat and Tall Organization Structure', in, *Administrative Science Quartely*, 14, pp. 178–191.

13 Charan, R., September–October 1991, 'How Networks Reshape Organizations For Results', in, *Harvard Business Review*, pp. 104–115.

14 Child, J., 1984, *Organisation*, Harper and Row, London.

15 Daems, H., and S.W. Douma, 1989, *Concurrentiestrategie en concernstrategie*, Kluwer Bedrijfswetenschappen, Deventer.

16 Dale, D., December 1989, 'Organising for Economy', in, *Australian Accountant*, pp. 76–79.

17 Dikstaal, N., and H. van Snellenberg, May 1992, 'Marktpositie dicteert stuurvariabelen', in, *Rendement*, pp. 60–64.

18 Dore, R.P., *et al.*, 1989, *Japan at Work, Markets Management, and Flexibility*, OECD, Paris.

19 Dore, R.P., 1973, *British Factory–Japanese Factory: The origins of diversity in industrial relations*, University of Califomia Press, Berkeley, CA.

20 Drucker, P.F., January–February 1988, 'The Coming of the New Organization', in, *Harvard Business Review*, pp. 45–53.

21 Drucker, P.F., September–October 1992, 'The New Society of Organisations', in, *Harvard Business Review*, pp. 95–104.

22 El Salmi, A.M., and L.L. Cummings, 1968, 'Managers' Perceptions of Needs and Need Satisfaction as a Function of Interactions Among Organizational Variables', in, *Personnel Psychology*, 21, pp. 465–477.

23 Farris, G.F., 1969, 'Organizational Factors and Individual Performance: a Longitudinal Study', in, *Journal of Applied Psychology*, 53, 2, pp. 87–92.

24 French, W.L., F.E. Kast and J.E. Rosenzweig, 1985, *Understanding Human Behaviour in Organizations*, Harper and Row, New York.

25 Gannon, M.J., and F.T. Paine, 1974, 'Unity of Command and Job Attitudes of Managers in a Bureaucratic Organization', in, *Journal of Applied Psychology*, 59, 3, pp. 392–394.

26 Ghiselli, E.E., and D.A. Johnson, 1970, 'Need Satisfaction, Managerial Success and Organizational Structure', in, *Personnel Psychology*, 23, pp. 569–576.

27 Ghiselli, E.E., and J.P. Siegel, 1972, 'Leader and Managerial Success in Tall and Flat Organization Structures', in, *Personnel Psychology*, 25, pp. 617–624.

28 Gunther, K., November 1989, 'The Horizontal Organization', in, *Executive Excellence*, 6, pp. 3–5.

29 Handy, C., and A. Tank (Ed), 1989, *From Hierarchy to Network*, The Conference Board Europe, Research Monograph No. 2, Brussels.

30 Harrison, R., September–October, 1972, 'How to Describe Your Organisation', in, *Harvard Business Review*.

33 Herbst, Ph.G., 1976, *Alternatives to Hierarchies*, Nijhoff, Leiden.

32 Hickson D.J., *et al.*, 1969, 'Operations Technology and Organization Structure: An Empirical Reappraisal', in, *Administrative Science Quarterly*, pp. 37X–399.

33 Hofstede, G., 1980, *Culture's Consequences: International differences in work-related values*, SAGE Publications, Beverly Hills.

34 Hofstede, G., 1991, *Allemaal andersdenkenden: omgaan met cultuurverschillen*, Contact, Amsterdam.

35 Horovitz, J.H., 1978, 'Management Control in France Great Britain and Germany', in, *Columbia Journal of World Business*, 13, 2, pp. 16–22.

36 In 't Veld, J., 1985, *Organisatiestructuur en arbeidsplaats: de organisatie van mensen en middelen; theorie en praktijk*, Elsevier, Amsterdam/Brussels.

37 Inkson, J.H.K., D.S. Pugh and D.J. Hickson, 1970, 'Organization Context and

Structure, an Abbreviated Replication', in, *Administrative Science Quarterly*, 15, pp. 318–329.

38 Ivancevich, J.M., and J.H. Donnelly, 1975, 'Relation of Organizational Structure to Job Satisfaction Anxiety–Stress and Performance', in, *Administrative Science Quarterly*, 20, pp. 272–280.

39 Jacques, E., January–February 1990, 'In Praise of Hierarchy', in: *Harvard Business Review*, pp. 127–133.

40 Janger, A., 1989, *Measuring Managerial Layers and Spans*, The Conference Board Europe, Research Bulletin No. 237. Brussels.

41 Keuning, D., and D.J. Eppink, 1990 (4th revised edition), *Management en Organisatie: Theorie en Toepassing*, Stenfert Kroese, Leiden.

42 Kimberly, J.R., and R.E. Quinn, *New futures: The challenge of managing corporate transitions*, Dow Jones, Irwin, Homewood, Illinois.

43 Kor, R., M. Weggeman and G. Wijnen, 1992, *De motivatie van de manager*, Twijnstra Gudde/Kluwer Bedrijfswetenschappen, Amersfoort/Deventer.

44 Kruger, W., and S. Reiszner, 1990. 'Inhaltsmuster der Hierarchie', in, *Organisation*, 6, pp. 380–388.

45 Lawler III, E.E., 1988, 'Substitutes for Hierarchy', in, *Organizational Dynamics*, 17, pp. 4–15.

46 Lawler III, E.E., November 1990, 'Making Your Firm More Competitive', in, *Executive Excellence*, 7, pp. 9–10.

47 Lincoln, J.R., *et al.*, 1986, 'Organisational Structures in Japanese and US Manufacturing', in, *Administrative Science Quarterly*, 31, pp. 338–364.

48 Lorsch, J.W., and J.J. Morse, 1974, *Organizations and Their Members: A Contingency approach*, Harper and Row, New York.

49 Luke, R.A., jun., *et al.*, 1973, 'A Structural Approach to Organisational Change', in, *Journal of Applied Behavioural Science*, 9, 5, pp. 611–635.

50 McMahon, J.T. and J.M. Ivancevich, March 1976, 'A Study of Control in a Manufacturing Organization: Managers and Non-managers', in, *Administrative Science Quarterly*, 21, pp. 66–83.

51 McMahon, J.T., 1976, 'Participative and Power-Equalized Organizational Systems: An Empirical Investigation and Theoretical Integration', in, *Human Relations*, 29, 3, pp. 203–214.

52 Meltzer, L., and J. Salter, 1962, 'Organizational Structure and the Performance and Job Satisfaction of Physiologists' in, *American Sociological Review*, 27, pp. 135–148.

53 Naber, J.L.G., February 1992, 'Organisatieverandering: bewegen en bewogen worden', *B&id*, pp. 12–20.

54 Neghandhi, A.R., and S.B. Prasad, 1971, *Comparative Management*, Appleton-Century-Crofts, New York.

55 Nelson, R.E., August 1988, 'Commonsense Staff Reduction', in, *Personnel Journal*, pp. 50–57.

56 O'Connell, M.J., L.L. Cummings and G.P. Huber, 1976, 'The Effects of Environmental Information and Decision Unit Structure on Felt Tension', in, *Journal of Applied Psychology*, 61, 4, pp. 493–500.

57 Ostroff, F. and D. Smith, 1992, 'The Horizontal Organisation', in, *The McKinsey Quarterly*, pp. 148–167.

58 Porter, L.W., and E.E. Lawler III, 1965, 'Properties of Organization Structure in Relation to Job Attitudes and Job Behaviour', in, *Psychological Bulletin*, 64, 1, pp. 23–51.

59 Porter, L.W., and E.E. Lawler III, 1964, 'The Effects of Tall vs. Flat Organizational Structures on Managerial Job Satisfaction', in, *Personnel Psychology*, 17, pp. 135–148.

60 Porter, L.W., and E.E. Lawler III, 1965, 'Properties of Organization Structure in Relation to Job Attitudes and Job Behaviour', in, *Psychological Bulletin*, 64, I, pp. 23–51.

61 Pugh, D.S., *et al.*, 1969, 'The Context of Organization Structures', in, *Administrative Science Quartely*, 14, pp. 91–114.

62 Quinn Mills, D., 1992, 'The Truth About Empowerment', in, *Training & Development*, pp. 31–32.

63 Quinn, J.B., and P.C. Paquett, Winter 1990, 'Effective Service Automation Generally Encourages Greater – Rather Than Less – Empowerment and Decentralization at the Contact Level', in, *Sloan Management Review*, pp. 69–78.

64 Reiss, M., 1992, 'Met bloed, zweet en tranen naar de slanke organisatie', in, *PEM*, 8, 3, pp. 407–414.

65 Roele, B., 18 January 1992, 'Chefs in de knel', in, *Elsevier Magazine*, pp. 46–50.

66 Rubenstein, A.H., 1988., *Managing Technology in the Decentralized Form*, Wiley, New York.

67 Schein, E.H., Winter 1989, 'Reassessing the "Divine Rights" of Managers', in, *Sloan Management Review*, 30, pp. 63–68.

68 Schlesinger, L.A., and J.L. Heskett, September–October 1991, 'The Service-driven Service Company', in, *Harvard Business Review*, pp. 71–81.

69 Schoemaker, M.J.R., and Th.D. Geerdink, 1991, *Human talent management: een visie op besturen, faciliteren en ontwikkelen van personeel*, Kluwer, Bedrijfswetenschappen, Deventer.

70 Schuring, R.W., 1992, 'De relatie van het organisatie-ontwerp van autonome taakgroepen met de kwaliteit van de arbeid en de groepsoutput', in, *Bedrijfskunde*, 64, 2, pp. 134–142.

71 Scott, D.S., and D.T. Jaffe, 1991, *Empowerment: Building a Committed Workforce*, Kogan Page, London.

72 Sitter, L.U., December 1987, *Op weg naar nieuwe fabrieken en kantoren*, Kluwer, Bedrijfswetenschappen, Deventer.

73 Stewart, T.A., 18th May 1992, 'The Search for the Organization of Tomorrow', in, *Fortune*, pp. 67–72.

74 Tank, A., 1991, *The Role of the Centre: New linkages in fast changing companies*. The Conference Board Europe, Research Monograph, No. 6, Brussels.

75 Trompenaars, F., z.j. *The Organization of Meaning and the Meaning of Organization*, The P.A. Whanton School.

76 Vancil, R.F., 1979, *Decentralization: Managerial Ambguity by Design: A research study and report*, Dow Jones, Irwin, Homewood, Illinois.

77 Venekamp, G., 1992, 'Bij het middenkader gaan harde klappen vallen', in, *Bedrijfsdocumentaire*, 5, 5, pp. 18–20.

78 Verhoeven, W., 1991, *Managen zonder hiërarchie*, Nelissen, Baarn.

79 Versteeg, F., 25 August 1992, 'Saturn breekt rigoureus met GM traditie', in, *NRC Handelsblad*, pp. 11–12.

80 Weggeman, M., G. Wijnen and R. Kor, 1985, *Ondernemen binnen de onderneming*, Kluwer, Bedrijfswetenschappen, Deventer.

81 Weixel, S., 20 August 1990, '*Flat Management Requires Juggling*', in, *Computerworld*, 24, pp. 70–71.

82 Whisler, T.L., 1970, *The Impact of Computers on Organizations*, MIT Press, Cambridge, MA.

83 Whyte, W.F., and R.A. Webber, 1969, *Culture and Management*, Dow Jones, Irwin, Homewood, Illinois.

84 Wieringa, P.A., April 1992, 'Top wordt kopje kleiner', in, *FEM*, pp. 56–60.

85 Wijnen, G., R. Kor and M. Weggeman, 1988, *Verbeteren en vernieuwen van organisaties, ook werk voor managers*, Kluwer, Bedrijfswetenschappen, Deventer.

86 Wissema, J.G., H.M. Messer and G.J. Wijers, 1986, *Angst voor veranderen? Een mythe?*, Van Gorcum, Assen.

87 Wissema, J.G., 1987, *Unit Management*, Van Gorcum, Assen.

88 Woodward, J., 1968, *Industrial Organization: Theory and practice*, Oxford University Press, London.

89 Worthy, J.C., 1950, 'Organizational Structure and Employee Morale', in, *American Sociological Review*, 15, pp. 169–179.

90 In own adaptation of *Part One: The Concept and Techniques of Strategic Management*, Chapter 9.

91 Reference to Quinn Mills, *Rebirth of the Corporation*, cited in, Peters, T., 1992, *Liberation Management*, MacMillan, London.

Additional references in the English language edition.

92 Abegglen, J.C., and G. Stalk, jun., 1985, *Kwisha: The Japanese corporation*, Basic Books Inc., New York.

93 Aguilar, Professor F.J., and Professor R. Hamermesh, 1981, *General Electric: Strategic position 1981*, Harvard Business School, Case No. 381–174.

94 Anonymous, 30 March 1991, 'Jack Welch reinvents General Electric – again', in: *The Economist*.

95 Anonymous, 25 January 1993, 'Jack Welch's lessons for success', in, *Fortune*, pp. 86–93.

96 Azumi, K., and C. McMillan, 1981. 'Management Strategy and Organization Structure: A Japanese Comparative Study', in, D.J. Hickson and C. McMillan. *Organization and Nation: The Aston Programme IV*, Gower, Aldershot, Great Britain.

97 Bossidy, L.A., November 1990, 'New ways of working together', in, *Executive Speeches*,

98 Chandler, A.D, jun., 1991, 'The functions of the HQ unit in the multi-business firm', in, *Strategic Management Journal*, 12, pp. 31–50.

99 The Conference Board Europe, 1992, *The Role of the Centre: New linkages in fast changing companies*.

100 Crozier, M., 1964, *The Bureaucratic Phenomenon*, University of Chicago Press, Chicago.

101 Daft, R.L., 1992, *Organization Theory and Design*, West Publishing Company.

102 Goold, M. and A.Campbell, 1987, *Strategies and Styles: The role of the centre in diversified corporations*, Basil Blackwell, Oxford.

103 Haire, M., E.E. Ghiselli and L.W. Porter, 1968, *Managerial Thinking: An international study*, Wiley, New York.

104 Inkson, J.H.K., *et al.*, 1970, 'A Comparison of Organization Structure and Managerial Roles: Ohio, USA and the Midlands, England', in, *The Journal of Management Studies*.

105 Koerner, E., 'GE's high-tech strategy', in, *Long Range Planning*, 22, 4, pp. 11–19.

106 Peters, T., 1992, *Liberation Management*, Alfred A. Knopf, New York.

107 Rapoport, C., 29 June 1992, 'How Barnevik makes ABB work', in, *Fortune*,

108 Sherman, S.P., 27 March, 1989, 'Inside the mind of Jack Welch', in, *Fortune*, pp. 37–44.

109 Slater, R., 1993, *The New GE: How Jack Welch revived an American institution*, Business One, Irwin, Homewood, Illinois.

110 Stewart, Th. A., 12 August 1991, 'GE keeps those ideas coming', in, *Fortune*,

111 Taylor, W., March–April 1991, 'The logic of Global Business', in, *Harvard Business Review*,

112 Tichy, N.M. and S. Sherman, 1993, *Control Your Destiny or Somebody Else Will: How Jack Welch is making General Electric the world's most competitive corporation*, Currency Doubleday.

113 Tichy, N., and R. Charan, September/October 1989, 'Speed, simplicity, self confidence: An interview with Jack Welch', in, *Harvard Business Review*, pp.112–121.

114 Yoshino, M.Y., 1968, *Japan's Managerial System: Tradition and innovation*, MIT Press, Cambridge, MA.

INDEX